21 Fun Songs to Teach French Phonics

Sing and Dance your Way to Perfect Pronunciation

2nd edition

Catherine Cantin and Laura Maddock

For instructions on how to download your free digital files, please see page 107.

We hope you and your pupils enjoy using the songs and ideas in this book. Brilliant Publications publishes many other books to help teach MFL in primary schools. To find out more details on all of our titles, including those listed below, please go to our website: www.brilliantpublications.co.uk.

Title	ISBN
100+ Fun Ideas for Practising Modern Foreign Languages in the Primary Classroom	978-1-903853-98-6
100+ Fun Ideas for Teaching French Across the Curriculum	978-1-905780-79-2
12 Mini French Plays	978-1-78317-360-0
Bonne Idée	978-1-905780-62-4
C'est Français	978-1-903853-02-3
Chantez Plus Fort	978-1-903853-37-5
French Festivals and Traditions	978-1-905780-44-0
French is Fun at Key Stage 1	978-0-85747-830-6
French Pen Pals Made Easy	978-1-905780-10-5
French Speaking Activities	978-1-905780-66-2
Hexagonie, Part 1	978-1-905780-59-4
Hexagonie, Part 2	978-1-905780-18-1
J'aime Chanter	978-1-905780-11-2
J'aime Parler	978-1-905780-12-9
Jouons Tous Ensemble	978-1-903853-81-8
Learn French through Raps	978-0-85747-691-3
Learn French with Luc et Sophie, 1ère Partie Starter Pack, Years 3–4	978-1-78317-343-3
Learn French with Luc et Sophie, 2ème Partie Starter Pack, Years 5–6	978-1-78317-344-0
Loto Français	978-1-905780-45-7
More Fun Ideas for Advancing Modern Foreign Languages in the Primary Classroom	978-1-905780-72-3
Petites Étoiles	978-0-85747-851-1
Physical French Phonics	978-0-85747-958-7
Unforgettable French	978-1-78317-093-7

Published by Brilliant Publications Limited
Unit 10
Sparrow Hall Farm
Edlesborough
Dunstable
Bedfordshire
LU6 2ES, UK

www.brilliantpublications.co.uk

Brilliant Publications is a registered trademark.

Written by Catherine Cantin and Laura Maddock
Illustrated by Gaynor Berry; coins artwork on page 45 designed by Freepik
Designed by Brilliant Publications Limited
Videos produced by Hart McLeod Limited
Songs written and sung by Catherine Cantin and composed and produced by Laura Maddock

© Brilliant Publications Limited 2021

Print ISBN: 978-1-78317-358-7
pdf ISBN: 978-1-78317-359-4

First printed and published in the UK in 2021.
2nd edition 2024
10 9 8 7 6 5 4 3 2 1

The right of Catherine Cantin and Laura Maddock to be identified as the authors of this work has been asserted by them in accordance with the Copyright, Designs and Patents Act 1988.

All rights reserved. Apart from any use permitted under UK copyright law, no part of this publication may be reproduced or transmitted in any form or by any means, electronic or mechanical, including photocopying and recording, or held within any information storage and retrieval system, without permission in writing from the publishers or under licence from the Copyright Licensing Agency Limited. Further details of such licenses (for reprographic reproduction) may be obtained from the Copyright Licensing Agency Limited, 5th Floor, Shackleton House, 4 Battle Bridge Lane, London SE1 2HX (https://cla.co.uk).

Contents

	page
Phonics focus for each song	4
About the authors	6
Introduction	7
How to use this resource	8

Songs

	French song title	English song title	Key phoneme(s)	Page
1.	Il y a quelqu'**un** ?	Is anybody there?	un	10
2.	Mon cachal**ot**	My whale	o / eau	14
3.	Mon petit l**ou**p	My little wolf	ou	18
4.	Une arai**gn**ée dans ma bai**gn**oire	A spider in my bathtub	gn	22
5.	L**u**l**u** la tort**u**e	Lulu the turtle	u	26
6.	Le rock 'n' roll du coch**on**	The piggy rock 'n' roll	on	30
7.	Mon ami Jul**ien**	My friend Julien	ien	34
8.	Le **ch**at en **ch**ocolat	The cat made out of chocolate	ch	38
9	Il y a une petite b**ê**te	There is a little bug	ê / è	42
10.	Petit **en**f**an**t	Little child	en / an	46
11.	Fran**ç**ois le **s**erpent	François the snake	ç / s / ss	50
12.	**Ga**ston le **go**rille	Gaston the gorilla	go / ga / gu	54
13.	**Gi**gi et **Ge**orges	Gigi and Georges	gi / ge / gé	58
14.	Chlo**é** et Barnab**é**	Chloe and Barnaby	é / er	62
15.	Du lund**i** au d**i**manche	From Monday to Sunday	i	66
16.	Papy, raconte-m**oi** une hist**oi**re !	Grandpa, tell me a story!	oi	70
17.	Une glace à la van**ille**	Vanilla ice cream	ille	74
18.	Le rap du hérisson	The hedgehog rap	silent h	78
19.	**Qu**'est-ce **qu**e … ?	What …?	qu	82
20.	Troi**s** oi**s**eaux	Three birds	s pronounced as z	86
21.	Le petit canard **Coin**-**coin**	Quack-quack the little duck	oin	90

	page
French phonics progress chart	94
Teaching ideas	95
Translation of assessment phrases on worksheets and PowerPoint	99
Translation of word lists on PowerPoint	101
Worksheet answers	105
Instructions for downloading the digital files	107

Phonics focus for each song

Grapheme	Song title	Image	Other examples from the song	Page numbers
un	Il y a quelqu'un ?	un	quelqu'un, brun Note: 'um' also makes this phonic sound: parfum.	10–13 (Tracks 1 & 22)
o/eau	Mon cachalot	cachalot	seau, eau, gros, beau Note: 'au' and 'ô' also make this phonic sound: jaune, hôtel.	14–17 (Tracks 2 & 23)
ou	Mon petit loup	loup	où, doux, joue, gadoue, hibou, toujours, nous, chouette	18–21 (Tracks 3 & 24)
gn	Une araignée dans ma baignoire	araignée	baignoire, mignon	22–25 (Tracks 4 & 25)
u	Lulu la tortue	tortue	Lulu, univers, fusée, lune, Neptune, revenue, sur	26–29 (Tracks 5 & 26)
on	Le rock 'n' roll du cochon	cochon	bonbon, mouton, gazon, lion, violon, poisson, pantalon, hérisson, avion, mignon Note: 'om' also makes this phonic sound: ombre, combien.	30–33 (Tracks 6 & 27)
ien	Mon ami Julien	chien	Julien, rien, bien	34–37 (Tracks 7 & 28)
ch	Le chat en chocolat	chat	chocolat, chasser, chaud Note: Each verse has a different vowel sound: a like in 'chat' e like in 'heureux' i like in 'ami' o like in 'l'eau' u like in 'disparu'	38–41 (Tracks 8 & 29)
ê/è	Il y a une petite bête	bête	fête, tête, pète Note: 'ai' and 'ei' also make this phonic sound: lait, seize.	42–45 (Tracks 9 & 30)
en/an	Petit enfant	enfant	maman, demande, grand, autant Note: 'em' and 'am' also make this phonic sound: décembre, champagne.	46–49 (Tracks 10 & 31)

Grapheme	Song title	Image	Other examples from the song	Page numbers
ç/s/ss	François le serpent	caleçon	François, serpent, garçon, essaye Note: see also 's sounds like z' (page 86–89).	50–53 (Tracks 11 & 32)
go/ga/gu	Gaston le gorille	gorille	Gaston, guitare, fatigué, godasses Note: see also 'gi/ge/ge' (page 58–61).	54–57 (Tracks 12 & 33)
gi/ge/gé	Gigi et Georges	girafe	Gigi, Georges, géante Note: 'j' also makes this phonic sound: je, jour joli Note: see also 'go/ga/gu' (page 54–57).	58–61 (Tracks 13 & 34)
é/er	Chloé et Barnabé	éléphant	fée, école, vélo, aller, fusée Note: 'ez' makes the same phonic sound: le nez, taisez-vous! The word 'et' (and) also makes this phonic sound, although the letter string 'et' in other words (poulet, for example) does not.	62–65 (Tracks 14 & 35)
i	Du lundi au dimanche	ski	lundi, mardi, mercredi, jeudi, vendredi, samedi, dimanche, lit, riz, ski, fruits, merci, amis, différent Note: 'y' also makes this phonic sound: gymnastique, stylo.	66–69 (Tracks 15 & 36)
oi	Papy, raconte-moi une histoire !	histoire	moi, froid, noir, crois, couloir, rois, bois, loi, quoi, étoile, toi	70–73 (Tracks 16 & 37)
ille	Une glace à la vanille	brille	famille, fille, vanille	74–77 (Tracks 17 & 38)
silent h	Le rap du hérisson	hélicoptère	hérisson, Hervé, hôpital, Hector, hippo, Harry, hamster, hamburgers, histoire	78–81 (Tracks 18 & 39)
qu	Qu'est-ce que …?	qu'est-ce que	Examples from the worksheet: qui, quand, quel, est-ce que, pourquoi	82–85 (Tracks 19 & 40)
S sounds like Z	Trois oiseaux	oiseaux	fraises, raisins, cerises, bise Note: there are also examples of liaison in the song: vous êtes, vos ailes.	86–89 (Tracks 20 & 41)
oin	Le petit canard Coin-coin	Coin-coin	loin, foin, besoin	90–93 (Tracks 21 & 42)

21 Fun Songs to Teach French Phonics, 2nd edn
© Brilliant Publications Limited

About the authors

Catherine Cantin

Catherine obtained her First-Class Honours degree in English and French from the University of Warwick in 2003. She then moved to Paris where she worked for five years, before carrying out her PGCE in Modern Foreign Languages at the University of Exeter.

After obtaining her PGCE, she worked for five years as a secondary teacher of French and Spanish, before taking a break to have children.

After her second child was born, she set up her own business teaching French to babies, toddlers and their parents and grandparents. Teaching French through singing and dancing was a fantastic and transformative experience, and this led to Catherine's current role as Head of Modern Foreign Languages at an independent primary school in Worcestershire.

Making the most of children's natural enjoyment and enthusiasm for singing and dancing, Catherine has been able to hone her craft and create songs, poems and raps that capture the children's imagination and embed French vocabulary, phonics and grammar into their long-term memories.

Through the songs, gestures, videos and worksheets provided in this publication, Catherine hopes to pass on the flame of her passion and life-long love of learning languages.

Laura Maddock

With a childhood immersed in music, playing instruments and performance, Laura went on to gain a BA Hons at Bretton Hall, University of Leeds. Her career started by touring in the UK providing workshops in rap and break dancing, before becoming a piano and vocal coach in New York.

Laura then travelled around the world with her guitar and campervan called "Skippy"! During this time, she wrote songs and created a new technique for teaching music to pre-schoolers through story, dance and song.

After her travels Laura continued to train and work for the Technics Music Academy, Yamaha School of Music and Worcester Music Academy. Laura is now the Director of her own Music School in Worcester.

Laura's enthusiasm and love for playing music is infectious and her students have appeared on the TV, won awards at music festivals and together have raised thousands of pounds for local charities.

With Laura's international experiences of music she was able to bring different arrangements and styles to this fun and interactive French learning resource.

Introduction

Welcome to **21 Fun Songs to Teach French Phonics**! The 21 songs featured in this book have been purposefully written, each with a different French phonic focus. By using these songs and the accompanying worksheets, we guarantee a fun and interactive method to embed both French phonics and common vocabulary and phrases into your French curriculum.

Even before children are born, they are learning about sound, rhythm and language. Long before they can talk or walk, children are bathed in a world of movement and music, where they are sung to, cradled, rocked and bounced on their parents' knees in time to the beat of a nursery rhyme or lullaby. Learning language through music and movement is a very natural process to children, and we have endeavoured to emulate this process.

Once children have a basic grasp of oracy in their mother tongue, they are then taught a programme of phonics, to facilitate their ability to read and write. Sound and spelling links are the basic building blocks upon which a child's fluency is developed. We feel that it is as important, if not more so, to develop the same skills in second language acquisition.

Each of the songs is based on a different phoneme from the French language. This allows you to provide a specific phonic focus for your lesson. However, the lyrics have also been written with the primary MFL curriculum in mind, and so you will find a wealth of age-appropriate, frequently used vocabulary and phrases. The songs can therefore be used to reinforce different topics and units of work, as well as to focus on French phonics. The songs can be used throughout Key Stages 1 and 2, and many would be appropriate for revision in Key Stage 3.

Why is it important to teach phonics?
Phonics helps us to understand how letters come together to make different sounds. Teaching phonics helps learners to hear, identify and use different sounds, thus forming the basic foundations upon which reading, listening, writing and speaking skills are built. When teaching phonics, we refer to phonemes and graphemes.

- **Phoneme** – The smallest units of sound that make up spoken words
- **Grapheme** – The letter or group of letters that represent a sound. A grapheme can be thought of as the visual representation of a sound.

If we want our learners of French to be confident communicators, able to read aloud and speak with ease, to listen and understand, we must first provide them with a solid understanding of French phonics, and how it compares to English phonics. This will be key to unlocking their potential, their ability and their desire to communicate effectively in the target language and its importance cannot be underestimated.

We are confident that you and your pupils will enjoy singing, dancing and moving to these catchy French songs. We hope that you will also see the benefits in their oral, writing, listening and reading skills and, above all, in their confidence and motivation to communicate in French.

How to use this resource

This resource contains 21 French songs, specifically written and composed to facilitate the introduction and reinforcement of key phonic sounds at Key Stages 1 and 2. The resource will be invaluable for both specialist and non-specialist teachers of French.

The resource uses a multi-sensory approach to help pupils learn and remember French phonemes and the graphemes associated with them. Each song focuses on a specific phoneme, which is repeated frequently in the lyrics. To help embed correct pronunciation, a word, image and key gesture have been purposefully chosen for each phoneme. Children should be encouraged to copy the actions in the videos.

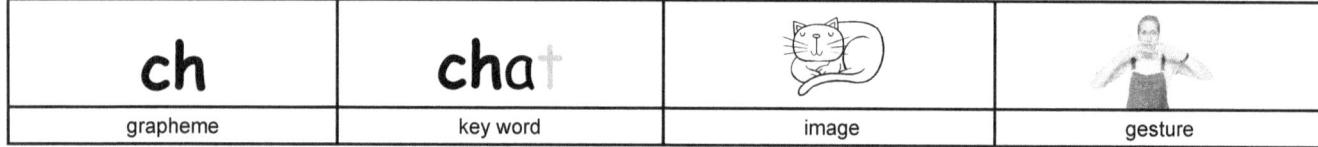

| grapheme | key word | image | gesture |

Silent letters in French

French words have a lot of silent letters, especially at the ends of words, and it can take some time for learners to get used to which letters they should and should not pronounce. To facilitate this task, we have put silent letters in grey in all oral tasks and activities in the book and its associated resources. We have tested this approach in the classroom and it has proven to be very effective.

In the free download files you will find:

❖ **Two videos** for each song, one with captions (eg 21FFS-V1-CAP.mp4) and one without (eg 21FFS-V1.mp4), so that pupils can read and listen to the words and watch and copy the actions. These will be invaluable for non-specialist teachers.

Video of song with captions

Video of song without captions

❖ **PowerPoint** (21FFS-PP.pptx) to allow the teacher to reinforce and revise key phonic sounds and/or assess their pupils' knowledge, understanding and retention. There are two slides for each of the 21 key phonic sounds included in the book. Slide 1 has an audio and a video file of the key phonic sound, for presentation, reinforcement and revision. Slide 2 has a sentence containing key words from the song. The sentence can be used for assessment purposes or for further reinforcement. There is also a list of words from the song containing the key phoneme and a list of other common words that contain the key phoneme. Again, these lists of words can be used for assessment or for further reinforcement.

PowerPoint Slide 1

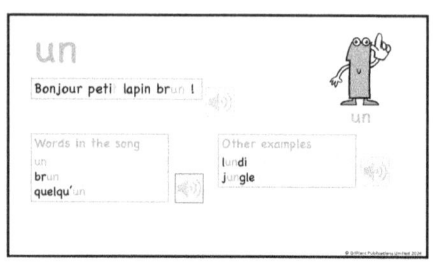
PowerPoint Slide 2

- ❖ **Flashcards** (21FFS-FC.pdf): these provide a screen-free option for presenting, revising and assessing the key phonic sound and its associated graphemes. Side A displays the key grapheme(s) for each phonic sound, as well as the key word and its associated image. Side B displays a list of words from the song containing the key graphemes. Teachers could show Side A and ask pupils to guess which words from the song might feature on Side B. Alternatively, the teacher could show the list of words on Side B and ask the pupils to tell them the key word and image on Side A. Teachers could also show side A and then ask pupils to read the words on Side B with the correct pronunciation. There are many different ways to use the flashcards!

Flashcard Side B   Flashcard Side A

- ❖ **Colour frieze** (21FFS-FRIEZE.pdf) of all the phonemes introduced, which can be printed out and displayed in the classroom. The frieze shows the key grapheme for each phoneme, as well as the key word and its associated image.

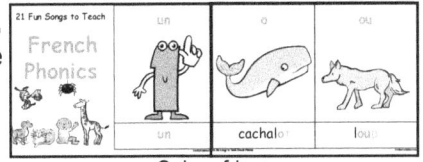
Colour frieze

- ❖ **French phonics chart** (21FFS-CHART.pdf). This chart can be printed out and displayed in the classroom. (If you are able to enlarge the charts to A3, this would be a bonus.)

- ❖ **Audio tracks** for all 21 songs (eg 21FFS-1-AUDIO.mp3)

- ❖ **Audio instrumental versions** of the songs, to enable 'karaoke' performances (eg 21FFS-22-AUDIO.mp3)

French phonics chart

In the book you will find:

- ❖ French lyrics page for each song. This doubles up as a colouring sheet for beginners

- ❖ English translations of the songs, enabling side-by-side comparison of the French and English lyrics

- ❖ Two worksheets for each song. Worksheets labelled A focus purely on embedding the key graphemes and phonemes and are for young and/or beginners. Worksheets labelled B provide a wider range of activities and exercises and are suitable for older and/or more confident learners

- ❖ Phonics focus for each song (pages 4–5), showing the graphemes associated with each phoneme, the song title, image and key word and other examples of the phoneme used in the song

- ❖ Teaching notes offering some additional ideas on how to exploit the songs and for possible extension work in the classroom and beyond (pages 95–98)

- ❖ French phonics progress chart (page 94). This can be photocopied and stuck in children's workbooks, to allow them to colour in each phoneme as they learn it and thus chart their progress.

- ❖ Answers for the worksheets. (pages 105–106)

Sample lyrics page   Sample English translation

Sample worksheet A

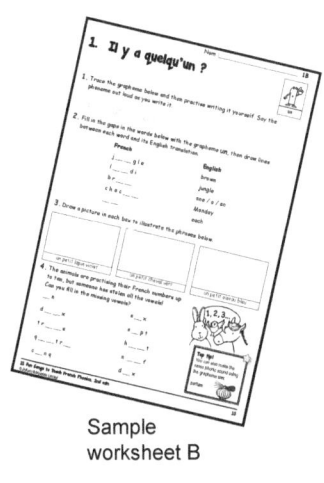

Sample worksheet B

21 Fun Songs to Teach French Phonics, 2nd edn

1. Il y a quelqu'un ?

Allô, allô !
Il y a quelqu'un ?

Oui, c'est moi ! Petit lapin brun !

Dansez, chantez, tapez, trois, deux, un
Dites bonjour à petit lapin brun.

Allô, allô !
Il y a quelqu'un ?

Oui, c'est moi ! Petit cheval brun !

Dansez, chantez, tapez, trois, deux, un
Dites bonjour à petit cheval brun.

Allô, allô !
Il y a quelqu'un ?

Oui, c'est moi ! Petit oiseau brun !

Dansez, chantez, tapez, trois, deux, un
Dites bonjour à petit oiseau brun.

1. Is anybody there?

un

Hello, hello!
Is anybody there?

Yes! It's me! Little brown rabbit!

Dance, sing, clap, three, two, one
Say hello to little brown rabbit.

Hello, hello!
Is anybody there?

Yes! It's me! Little brown horse!

Dance, sing, clap, three, two, one
Say hello to little brown horse.

Hello, hello!
Is anybody there?

Yes! It's me! Little brown bird!

Dance, sing, clap, three, two, one
Say hello to little brown bird.

Nom : _____ 1A

1. Il y a quelqu'un ?

un

1. Trace the grapheme below and then practise writing it yourself. Say the phoneme out loud as you write it.

un   un   un

2. Trace each word below and then practise writing it yourself. Say the word out loud as you write it.

un

lapin

cheval

oiseau

3. Colour in the picture below if you can read this sentence to a teacher or your partner. Watch out for silent letters in grey.

Bonjour petit lapin brun !

Nom :_____ 1B

1. Il y a quelqu'un ?

un

1. Trace the grapheme below and then practise writing it yourself. Say the phoneme out loud as you write it.

un   un   un

2. Fill in the gaps in the words below with the grapheme **un**, then draw lines between each word and its English translation.

French	English
j _ _ g l e	brown
l _ _ d i	jungle
b r _ _	one / a / an
c h a c _ _	Monday
_ _	each

3. Draw a picture in each box to illustrate the phrases below.

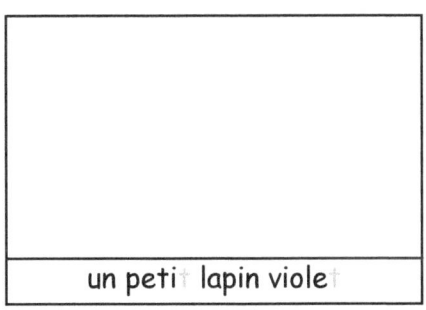
un petit lapin violet

un petit cheval vert

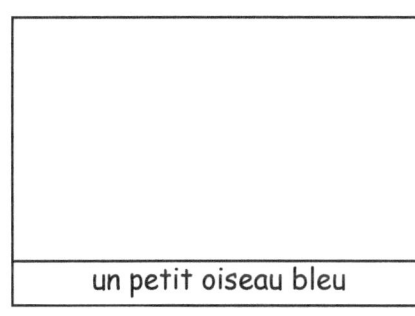
un petit oiseau bleu

4. The animals are practising their French numbers up to ten, but someone has stolen all the vowels! Can you fill in the missing vowels?

_ n   s _ x

d _ _ x   s _ p t

t r _ _ s   h _ _ t

q _ _ t r _   n _ _ f

c _ n q   d _ x

Top tip!
You can also make the same phonic sound using the grapheme **um**:

parfum

2. Mon cachalot

o/eau

J'ai un seau
Un joli seau
Dans mon seau
Il y a de l'eau.

J'ai un seau
Un joli seau
Dans mon seau
Il se cache un cachalot !

Un cachalot ?
Un cachalot !

Oooh là là, qu'il est gros !
Oooh là, là, qu'il est beau !
Mon cachalot
Plouf !

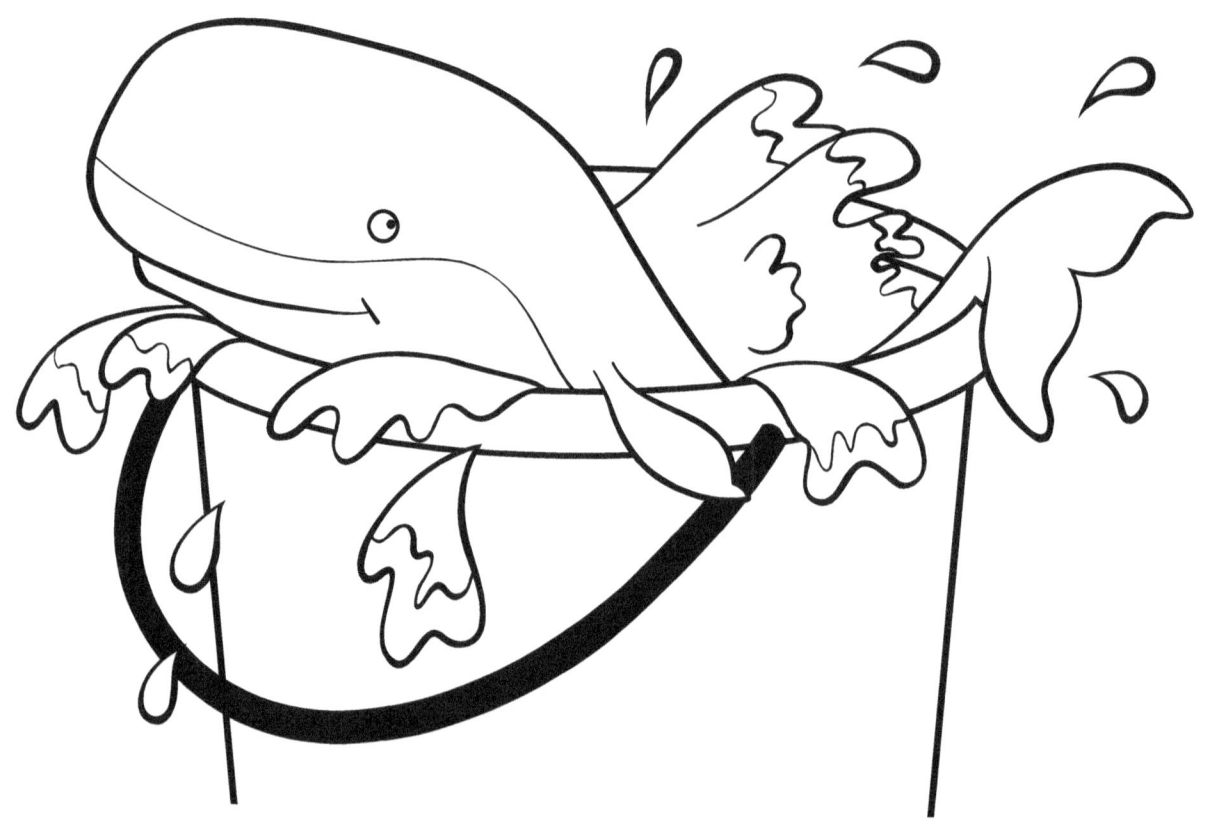

2. My whale

o/eau

I have a bucket
A lovely bucket
In my bucket
There is some water.

I have a bucket
A lovely bucket
In my bucket
A whale is hiding.

A whale?
A whale!

Wow! How big he is!
Wow! How handsome he is!
My whale
Splash!

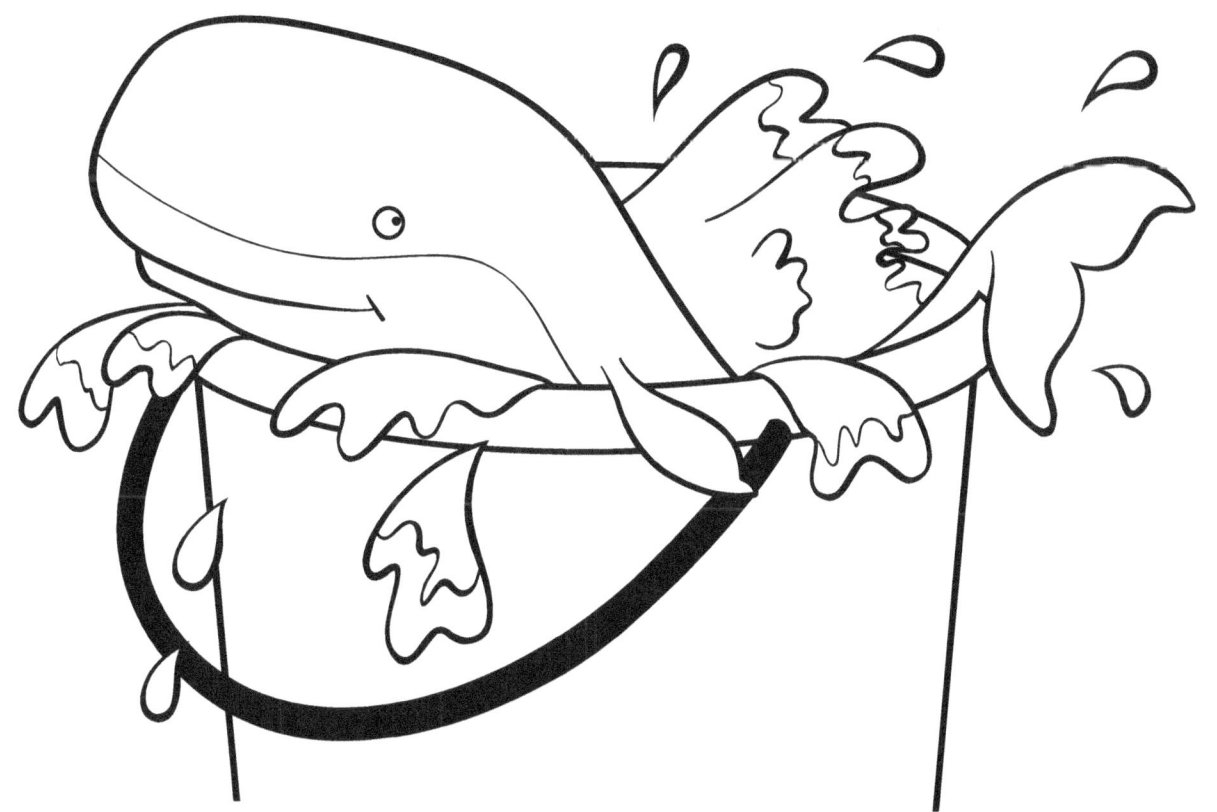

Nom : _____ 2A

2. Mon cachalot

o/eau

1. Trace the graphemes below and then practise writing them yourself. Say the phoneme out loud as you write it.

o   o   o   o

eau   eau

2. Trace each word below and then practise writing it yourself. Say the word out loud as you write it.

seau

cachalot

3. Colour in the picture below if you can read this sentence to a teacher or your partner. Watch out for silent letters in grey.

J'ai un gros cachalot dans mon seau !

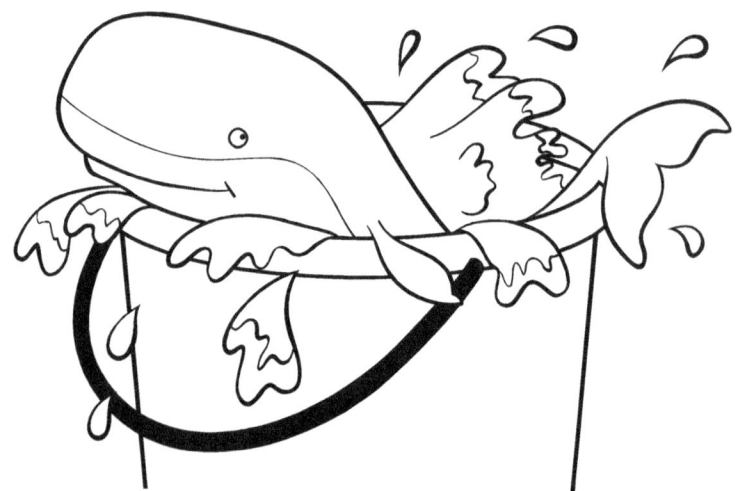

Nom :_____ 2B

2. Mon cachalot

Top tip!
The last letter in most French words is silent: cachalot, gros. Look out for other silent letters at the end of words!

o/eau

1. Trace the graphemes below and then practise writing them yourself. Say the phoneme out loud as you write it.

o   o   o   o

eau   eau

2. Circle the **four** words below that contain the grapheme **o** and rhyme with **cachalot**.

| dans   gros   gris   stylo   sac   dos   bleu   mot |

3. Circle the **four** words below that contain the grapheme **eau** and rhyme with **seau**.

| beurre   petit   couteau   feutre   bateau   beau   grand   chapeau |

4. Rearrange the syllables in the whale's spout to make the French word for whale. Write it in the sentence below.

Dans mon seau, il y a un __ __ __ __ __ __ __ __ .

5. Draw a picture of something you would like to find in your **seau**, then write a sentence about it in French. Can you add any extra details?

Dans mon seau il y a _____

_____

Top tip!
You can also make the same phonic sound using the following graphemes:
ô   hôtel (*hotel*)   au   jaune (*yellow*)

21 Fun Songs to Teach French Phonics, 2nd edn
© Brilliant Publications Limited
17

3. Mon petit loup

Où es-tu, mon petit loup,
Mon petit loup, tout doux ?

Moi, je joue dans la gadoue
Avec mon ami le hibou.

Où es-tu, mon petit loup,
Mon petit loup, tout doux ?

Moi, je joue dans la gadoue
Avec mon ami le hibou.

Mon petit loup
Tu ne m'aimes plus !
Toujours avec ton hibou !

Ne sois pas bête,
Fais pas la tête,
Viens faire la fête avec nous,
Viens faire la fête avec nous !

On fait la fête ?
Chouette !

3. My little wolf

ou

Where are you, my little wolf,
My little wolf, so soft?

I'm playing in the mud
With my friend, the owl.

Where are you, my little wolf,
My little wolf, so soft?

I'm playing in the mud
With my friend, the owl.

My little wolf
You don't love me anymore!
You're always with your owl!

Don't be silly!
Don't be mad!
Come and party with us,
Come and party with us!

We're having a party?
Great!

Nom :_____ 3A

3. Mon petit loup

ou

1. Trace the grapheme below and then practise writing it yourself. Say the phoneme out loud as you write it.

2. Trace each word below and then practise writing it yourself. Say the word out loud as you write it.

  loup

  hibou

 gadoue

3. Colour in the picture below if you can read this sentence to a teacher or your partner. Watch out for silent letters in grey.

Mon petit loup joue avec le hibou dans la gadoue.

Nom : _____ 3B

3. Mon petit loup

1. Trace the grapheme below and then practise writing it yourself. Say the phoneme out loud as you write it.

2. Draw a circle around every **ou** grapheme in the box below:

ou	oi	au	ou	oe	ou	oo	oa	ou	uo	ou	on
on	ou	oi	oo	ou	uo	ou	on	oi	ou	on	om

How many **ou** graphemes did you circle? ☐

3. Fill in the gaps in the words below with the grapheme **ou**, then draw lines between each word and the correct image.

l __ __ p   hib __ __

b __ __ le   gad __ __ e

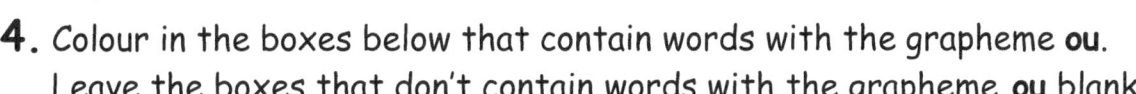

4. Colour in the boxes below that contain words with the grapheme **ou**. Leave the boxes that don't contain words with the grapheme **ou** blank.

fourmi	souris	journal	tortue
poule	bateau	douche	boîte
amour	bonbon	soupe	route

How many boxes did you colour in?

5. Imagine you are **petit loup**. What else do you play with your friend, **le hibou**? Finish off the sentence below in French. There are some ideas underneath to help you.

Je joue _____.

au rugby   au tennis   au foot   au basket   au hand

4. Une araignée dans ma baignoire

Il y a une araignée dans ma baignoire
Elle est poilue, grande et toute noire !
Je n'ai même pas peur, non, non, non,
Avoir une amie-araignée, c'est mignon.

C'est mignon, mignon, mignon, mignon
C'est mignon, mignon, mignon, mignon.

Il y a une araignée dans ma baignoire
Elle est poilue, grande et toute noire.
Je n'ai même pas peur, non, non, non,
Avoir une amie-araignée, c'est mignon !

C'est mignon, mignon, mignon, mignon
C'est mignon, mignon, mignon, mignon.

Et toi, tu aimes les araignées ?

4. A spider in my bathtub

gn

There is a spider in my bathtub
It's hairy, big and black all over!
I'm not even scared, no, no, no,
It's cute to have a spider as a friend.

It's cute, cute, cute, cute
It's cute, cute, cute, cute.

There is a spider in my bathtub
It's hairy, big and black all over!
I'm not even scared, no, no, no,
It's cute to have a spider as a friend.

It's cute, cute, cute, cute
It's cute, cute, cute, cute.

What about you? Do you like spiders?

Nom : _____ 4A

4. Une araignée dans ma baignoire

gn

1. Trace the grapheme below and then practise writing it yourself. Say the phoneme out loud as you write it.

gn   gn   gn

2. Trace each word below and then practise writing it yourself. Say the word out loud as you write it.

araignée

baignoire

montagne

3. Colour in the picture below if you can read this sentence to a teacher or your partner. Watch out for silent letters in grey.

Il y a une araignée dans ma baignoire.

Nom :_____ 4B

4. Une araignée dans ma baignoire

gn

1. Trace the grapheme below and then practise writing it yourself. Say the phoneme out loud as you write it.

gn   gn   gn

2. Circle the **four** words below that contain the grapheme **gn**.

montagne   plage   poignet   pigeon   cochon   mignon   baignoire

3. Practise saying the phrases below that contain words with the grapheme **gn**. Get your partner or teacher to listen to you and then tick the image when you are confident you can say the word correctly.

À la **campagne** il y a des **araignées** et des **champignons**.

Les **cygnes** volent en **ligne** vers les **montagnes**.

4. Draw **une araignée** in a **baignoire** below. Make sure your **araignée** is **poilue** (hairy), **grande** (big) and **toute noire** (black all over)!

5. Tu aimes les araignées ? (Do you like spiders?) Answer in French using phrases from the vocabulary box below.

_____

_____

_____

Vocabulary	
Oui	**Yes**
J'aime les araignées.	I like spiders.
Je n'ai pas peur des araignées.	I'm not afraid of spiders.
Non	**No**
Je n'aime pas les araignées.	I don't like spiders.
J'ai peur des araignées.	I'm afraid of spiders.

21 Fun Songs to Teach French Phonics, 2nd edn
© Brilliant Publications Limited

5. Lulu la tortue

Lulu la tortue
Un jour a décidé
De voyager à travers l'univers
Dans sa petite fusée.

5, 4, 3, 2, 1 – whoosh !

Elle a pique-niqué sur la lune

Elle a joué au foot sur Neptune

Et après ce voyage extraordinaire,
Tout doucement,
Tout doucement,
Tout doucement …
Elle est revenue sur la terre
Elle est revenue sur la terre.

5. Lulu the turtle

Lulu the turtle
Decided one day
To travel across the universe
In her little rocket.

5, 4, 3, 2, 1 – whoosh!

She had a picnic on the moon

She played football on Neptune

And after this extraordinary journey,
Very gently,
Very gently,
Very gently…
She came back down to Earth
She came back down to Earth.

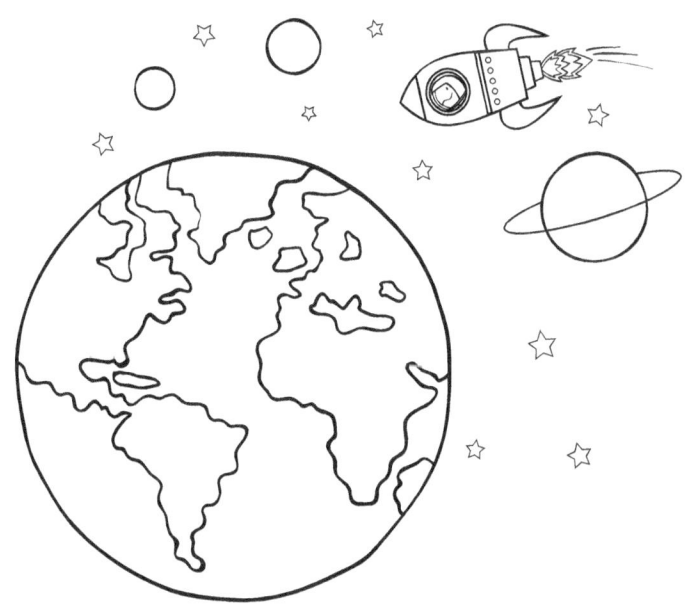

Nom :_____ 5A

5. Lulu la tortue

1. Trace the grapheme below and then practise writing it yourself. Say the phoneme out loud as you write it.

u   u   u   u

2. Trace each word below and then practise writing it yourself. Say the word out loud as you write it.

tortue

fusée

lune

3. Colour in the picture below if you can read this sentence to a teacher or your partner.

Lulu la tortue joue au foot sur Neptune.

Nom :_____ 5B

5. Lulu la tortue

u

1. Trace the grapheme below and then practise writing it yourself. Say the phoneme out loud as you write it.

u u u u

2. Draw pictures below to complete the comic strip about the adventures of **Lulu la tortue**, then read the comic strip out loud.

Lulu la tortue	un jour a decidé	de voyager à travers l'univers

dans sa petite fusée.	5, 4, 3, 2, 1 – whoosh !	Elle a pique-niqué sur la lune

	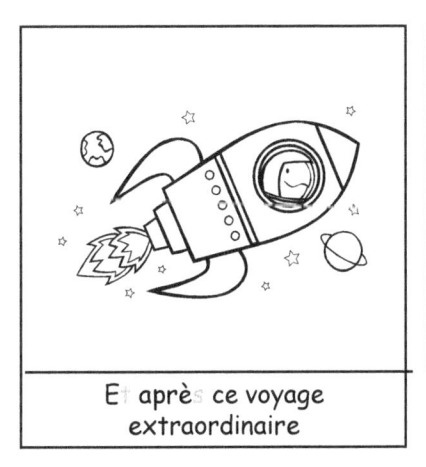	
elle a joué au foot sur Neptune.	Et après ce voyage extraordinaire	elle est revenue sur la terre.

tout doucement

21 Fun Songs to Teach French Phonics, 2nd edn
© Brilliant Publications Limited

6. Le rock 'n' roll du cochon

Venez, venez, on va chanter le rock 'n' roll des animaux !

Le rock 'n' roll des animaux
Le rock 'n' roll des animaux

Le cochon, le cochon, le cochon … mange des bonbons !

Le rock 'n' roll des animaux
Le rock 'n' roll des animaux

Le mouton, le mouton, le mouton … tond le gazon !

Le rock 'n' roll des animaux
Le rock 'n' roll des animaux

Le lion, le lion, le lion … joue du violon !

Le rock 'n' roll des animaux
Le rock 'n' roll des animaux

Le poisson, le poisson, le poisson … porte un pantalon !

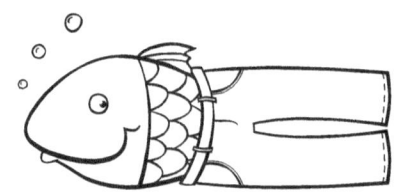

Le rock 'n' roll des animaux
Le rock 'n' roll des animaux

Le hérisson, le hérisson, le hérisson … pilote un avion !

Qu'est-ce qu'ils sont mignons !

6. The piggy rock 'n' roll

on

Roll up, roll up, we're going to sing the animal rock 'n' roll song!

The animal rock 'n' roll
The animal rock 'n' roll

The pig, the pig, the pig... is eating sweets!

The animal rock 'n' roll
The animal rock 'n' roll

The sheep, the sheep, the sheep... is mowing the lawn!

The animal rock 'n' roll
The animal rock 'n' roll

The lion, the lion, the lion... is playing the violin!

The animal rock 'n' roll
The animal rock 'n' roll

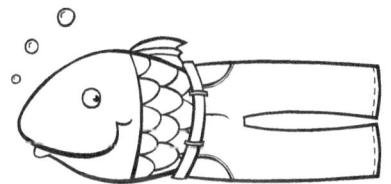

The fish, the fish, the fish... is wearing a pair of trousers!

The animal rock 'n' roll
The animal rock 'n' roll

The hedgehog, the hedgehog, the hedgehog... is flying an aeroplane!

They are so cute!

Nom : _____ 6A

6. Le rock 'n' roll du cochon

on

1. Trace the grapheme below and then practise writing it yourself. Say the phoneme out loud as you write it.

on   on   on

2. Trace each word below and then practise writing it yourself. Say the word out loud as you write it.

 cochon

 mouton

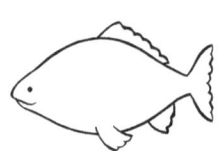 poisson

3. Colour in the picture below if you can read this sentence to a teacher or your partner. Watch out for silent letters in grey.

Le cochon mange des bonbons et le lion joue du violon !

Nom : _____ 6B

6. Le rock 'n' roll du cochon

on

1. Trace the grapheme below and then practise writing it yourself. Say the phoneme out loud as you write it.

2. Rearrange the letters in each animal below to spell out their name in French.

_____   _____   _____   _____   _____

3. Draw lines to match up the words with the correct images.

a) bonbon
b) gazon
c) violon
d) pantalon
e) avion

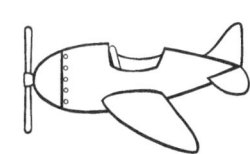

4. Draw pictures to illustrate the phrases in the boxes below:

Le cochon mange des bonbons.

Le poisson porte un pantalon.

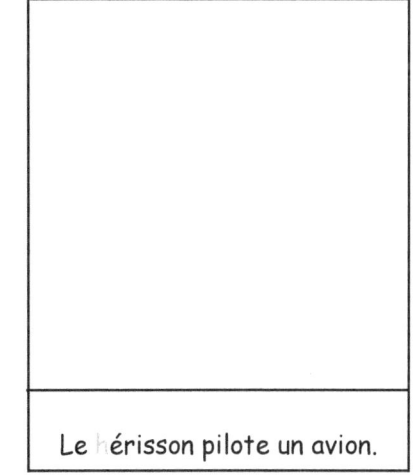
Le hérisson pilote un avion.

Top tip!
You can also make the same phonic sound using the grapheme **om**:
  ombre (*shadow*)   c**om**bien (*how much*)   b**om**be (*bomb*)   t**om**ber (*to fall*)

21 Fun Songs to Teach French Phonics, 2nd edn
© Brilliant Publications Limited

7. Mon ami Julien

J'ai un ami qui s'appelle Julien
Il aimerait un petit chien
Mais son père dit : non, non, non !

Ça ne sert à rien, d'avoir un petit chien
Quand tu as déjà un pingouin !

J'ai un ami qui s'appelle Julien
Il aimerait un petit chien
Mais son père dit : non, non, non !

Ça ne sert à rien, d'avoir un petit chien
Quand tu as déjà un babouin !

J'ai un ami qui s'appelle Julien
Il aimerait un petit chien
Mais son père dit : non, non, non !

Ça ne sert à rien, d'avoir un petit chien
Quand tu as déjà un requin !

Plutôt qu'un chien mon père
Pourquoi pas un petit frère ?

Finalement, mon Julien
Un petit chien, c'est très bien !

7. My friend Julien

ien

I have a friend called Julien
He would like a little dog
But his dad says: no, no, no!

There's no point having a little dog
When you already have a penguin!

I have a friend called Julien
He would like a little dog
But his dad says: no, no, no!

There's no point having a little dog
When you already have a baboon!

I have a friend called Julien
He would like a little dog
But his dad says: no, no, no!

There's no point having a little dog
When you already have a shark!

Rather than a dog, daddy dear,
How about a little brother?

On second thoughts Julien,
A little dog will be fine!

Nom : _____ 7A

7. Mon ami Julien

ien

1. Trace the grapheme below and then practise writing it yourself. Say the phoneme out loud as you write it.

   ien   ien   ien

2. Trace each word below and then practise writing it yourself. Say the word out loud as you write it.

   chien

   Julien

   bien

3. Colour in the picture below if you can read this sentence to a teacher or your partner. Watch out for silent letters in grey.

Mon ami Julien aimerait un petit chien.

Nom : _____ 7B

7. Mon ami Julien

ien

1. Trace the grapheme below and then practise writing it yourself. Say the phoneme out loud as you write it.

ien   ien   ien

2. Circle the **four** words below that contain the grapheme **ien** and rhyme with the word **Julien**.

(chat   chien   cheval   rien   rhino   bien   banane   magicien)

3. Draw pictures to illustrate the words in the boxes below:

un pingouin	un babouin	un requin

4. Choose some animals from the vocabulary box below that you would like to have, then complete the sentence below, starting 'J'aimerais' (I would like). The word for 'and' in French is 'et'.

J'aimerais _____

_____

_____

_____

Vocabulary

un éléphant	une girafe
un panda	une baleine
un lion	une tortue
un dauphin	une vache
un aigle	une araignée
un hippopotame	une souris

21 Fun Songs to Teach French Phonics, 2nd edn
© Brilliant Publications Limited

8. Le chat en chocolat

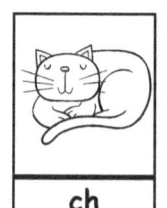

Tracks 8 & 29

ch

Top tip!
Each verse has a different vowel sound:
a like in 'ch**a**t'
e like in 'h**eu**r**eu**x'
i like in 'am**i**'
o like in 'l'**eau**
u like in 'dispar**u**'

Je vois le chat, chat, chat
En chocolat, lat, lat
Qui ne veut pas, pas, pas
Chasser le rat, rat, rat !

Je vois le chat, chat, chat
En chocolat, lat, lat
Qui mange des oeufs, oeufs, oeufs
Il est heureux, reux, reux !

Je vois le chat, chat, chat
En chocolat, lat, lat
Il me sourit, rit, rit
C'est mon ami, mi, mi !

Je vois le chat, chat, chat
En chocolat, lat, lat
Il boit de l'eau, l'eau, l'eau
Il a trop chaud, chaud, chaud !

Le petit chat, chat, chat
En chocolat, lat, lat
A disparu, ru, ru
Je suis déçu, çu, çu.

Mais non, je suis là ! Coucou !

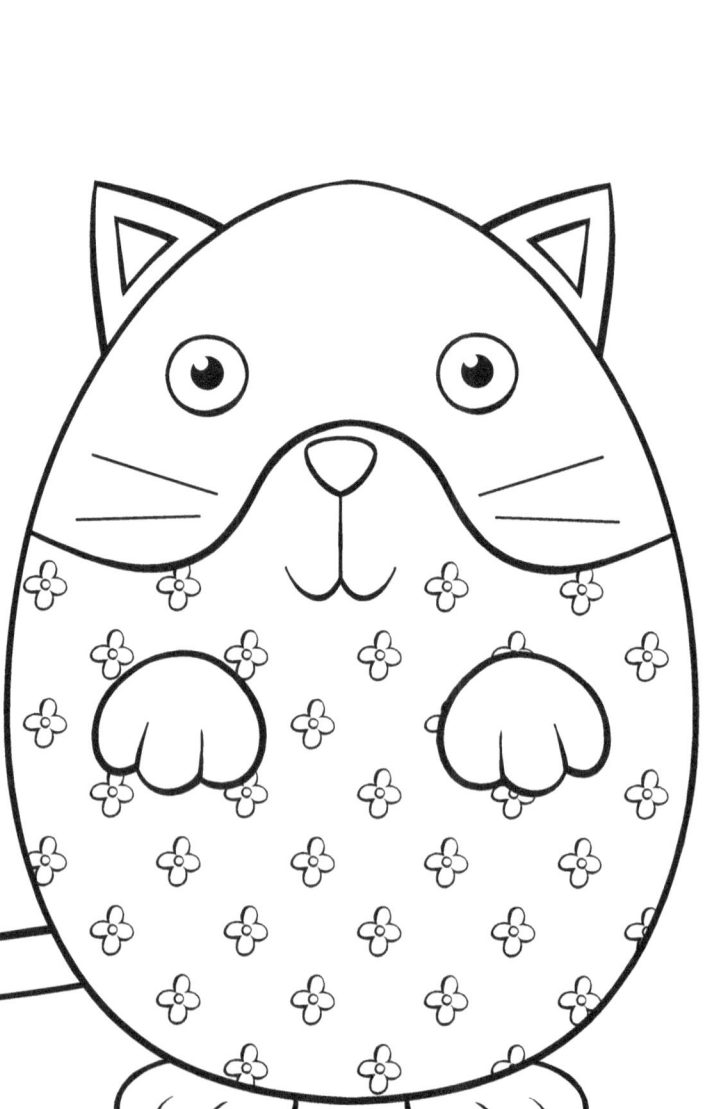

8. The cat made out of chocolate

I see the cat, cat, cat
Of chocolate, late, late
He doesn't want, want, want
To chase the rat, rat, rat!

I see the cat, cat, cat
Of chocolate, late, late
Eating eggs, eggs, eggs
He is happy, py, py!

I see the cat, cat, cat
Of chocolate, late, late
Smiling at me, me, me
He is my friend, friend, friend!

I see the cat, cat, cat
Of chocolate, late, late
Drinking water, ter, ter
He is too hot, hot, hot!

The little cat, cat, cat
Of chocolate, late, late
Has disappeared, peared, peared,
I'm disappointed, ted, ted.

No, I'm here! Coo-ey!

Nom : _____ 8A

8. Le chat en chocolat

1. Trace the grapheme below and then practise writing it yourself. Say the phoneme out loud as you write it.

   ch   ch   ch

2. Trace each word below and then practise writing it yourself. Say the word out loud as you write it.

   chat

   chocolat

   chaud

3. Colour in the picture below if you can read this sentence to a teacher or your partner. Watch out for silent letters in grey.

Le chat en chocolat boit un chocolat chaud !

Nom :_____ 8B

8. Le chat en chocolat

ch

1. Trace the grapheme below and then practise writing it yourself. Say the phoneme out loud as you write it.

   ch   ch   ch

2. Circle the **three** words below that rhyme with **chat**.

   (fromage   pas   maison   lundi   rat   œufs   chocolat)

3. Circle the word below that means 'happy' in French.

   (vois   mange   oeufs   heureux   chat   chasser)

4. How do we know that the chocolate cat is friendly? Circle the correct answer.

   (he wags his tail   he smiles   he purrs   he leaves presents)

5. What does the chocolate cat drink when he is too hot? Circle the correct answer.

   (milk   hot chocolate   water   lemonade   tea)

6. Which word describes how we feel when the chocolate cat disappears?

   (fâché   soulagé   déçu   heureux   fatigué   agacé)

7. Draw pictures to illustrate the following lines from the song:

   | Il mange des œufs. | Il me sourit. | Il a trop chaud. |

21 Fun Songs to Teach French Phonics, 2nd edn
© Brilliant Publications Limited

9. Il y a une petite bête

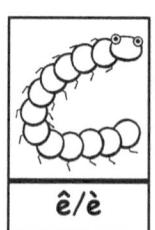

Il y a une petite bête
Qui fait la fête
Sur ma tête !
Il y a une petite bête
Qui fait la fête
Sur ma tête !

Elle danse, elle chante
À tue-tête !
Elle saute, elle crie
À tue-tête !
Il faudrait pas qu'elle pète !

Il y a une petite bête
Qui fait la fête
Sur ma tête !
Il y a une petite bête
Qui fait la fête
Sur ma tête !

Elle danse, elle chante
À tue-tête !
Elle saute, elle crie
À tue-tête !
Il faudrait pas qu'elle pète !

9. There is a little bug

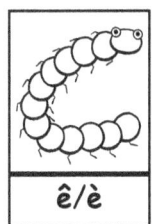

There is a little bug
Having a party
On my head!
There is a little bug
Having a party
On my head!

It's dancing, it's singing
At the top of its voice!
It's jumping, it's shouting
At the top of its voice!
It had better not trump!

There is a little bug
Having a party
On my head!
There is a little bug
Having a party
On my head!

It's dancing, it's singing
At the top of its voice!
It's jumping, it's shouting
At the top of its voice!
It had better not trump!

Nom : _____ 9A

9. Il y a une petite bête

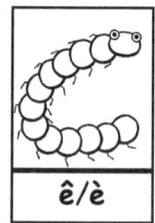
ê/è

1. Trace the graphemes below and then practise writing them yourself. Pay special attention to the accents. Say the phoneme out loud as you write it.

2. Trace each word below and then practise writing it yourself. Say the word out loud as you write it.

3. Colour in the picture below if you can read this sentence to a teacher or your partner.

La petite bête pète sur ma tête !

44   21 Fun Songs to Teach French Phonics, 2nd edn
© Brilliant Publications Limited

Nom : _____ 9B

9. Il y a une petite bête

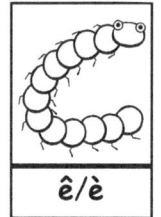
ê/è

1. Trace the graphemes below and then practise writing them yourself.
Pay special attention to the accents. Say the phoneme out loud as you write it.

2. Circle the **six** words below that contain the grapheme **ê**.

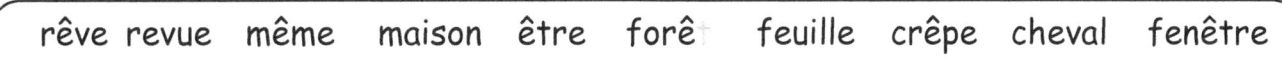
rêve   revue   même   maison   être   forêt   feuille   crêpe   cheval   fenêtre

3. Find and colour in the **four** mini beasts below that contain the grapheme **è**.

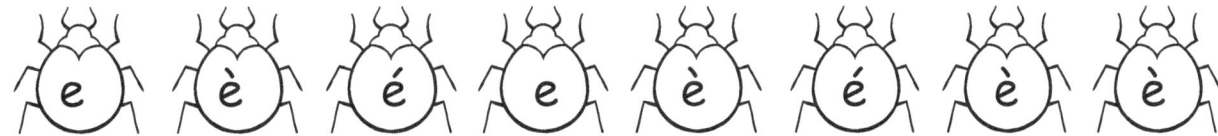
e   è   é   e   è   é   è   è

4. Draw pictures of the **petite bête** to illustrate the phrases below.

elle chante

elle saute

elle pète

Top tip!
'ai' and 'ei' also make this phonic sound:

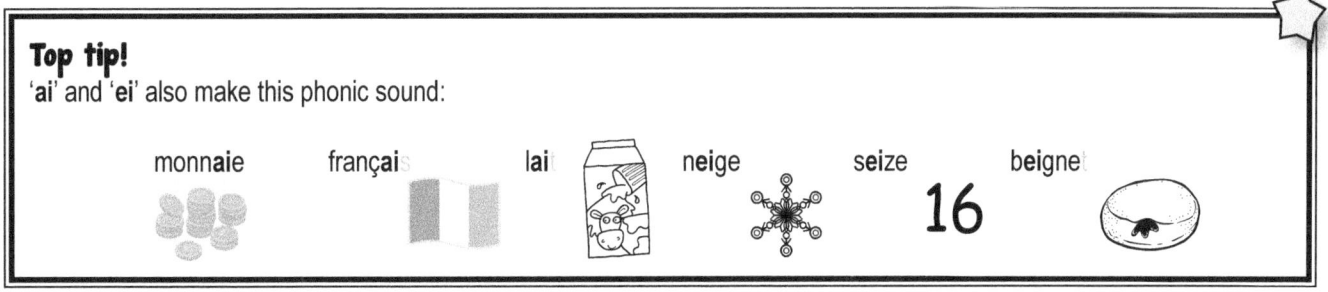
monnaie   français   lait   neige   seize   beignet

10. Petit enfant

en/an

Petit enfant
Aime sa maman
Et lui demande un jour :

Maman, maman
Quand serai-je grand ?
Je suis petit depuis si longtemps !

Petite maman
Aime son enfant
Et lui réponds toujours :

Ne t'inquiète pas, mon petit chat
Tu seras grand un jour, tu verras !
Mais d'ici là, reste comme ça
Je t'aimerai toujours.

Petit ou grand
Je t'aime autant
C'est pour la vie notre amour
C'est pour la vie notre amour.

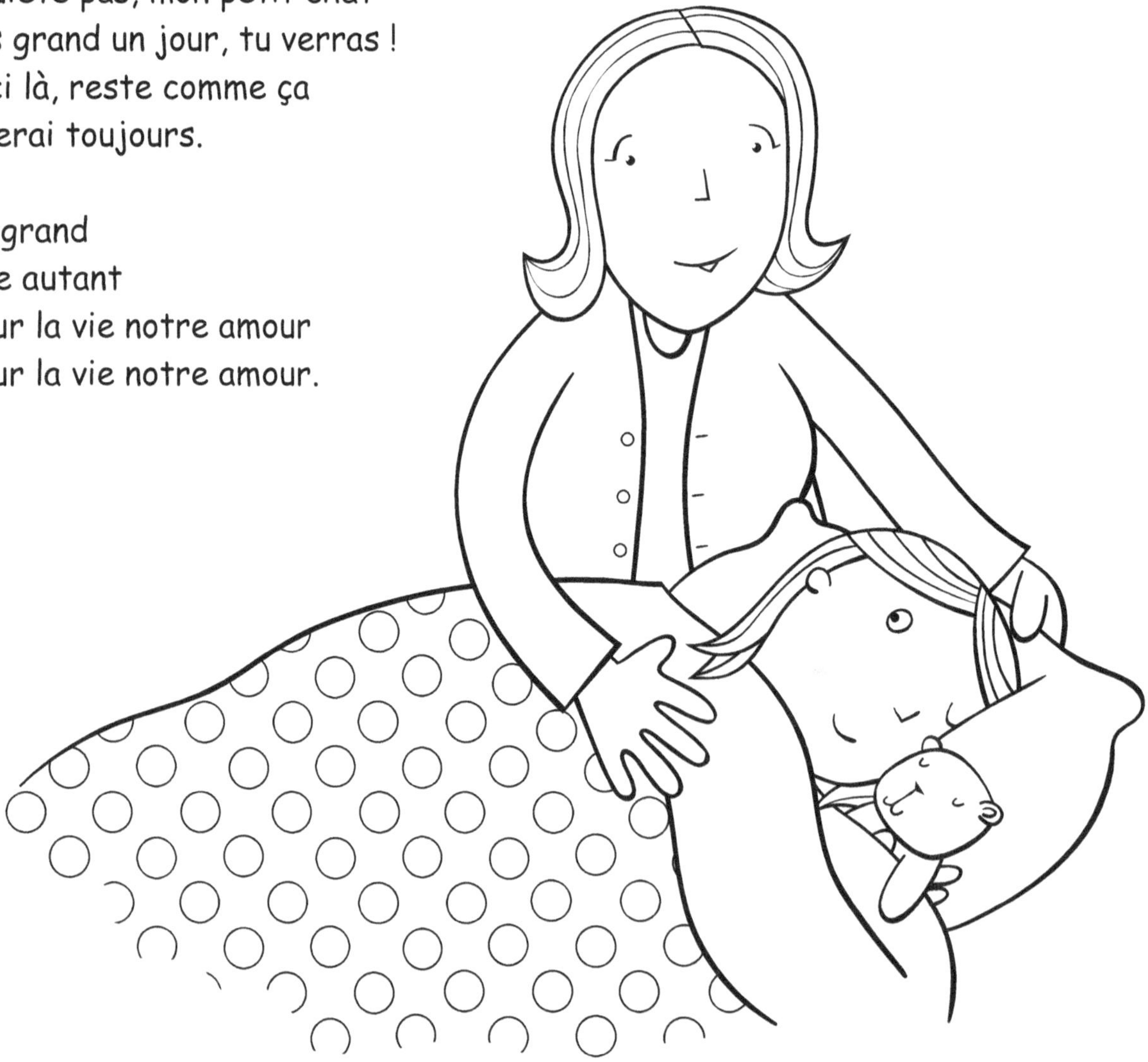

10. Little child

en/an

Little child
Loves his/her mother
And asks her one day:

Mummy, mummy,
When will I be big?
I have been little for such a long time!

Little mother
Loves her child so much
And always replies:

Don't worry, my little cat
You'll be big one day, you'll see!
Until then, stay as you are
I will always love you.

Little or big
I love you just the same
Our love will last forever
Our love will last forever.

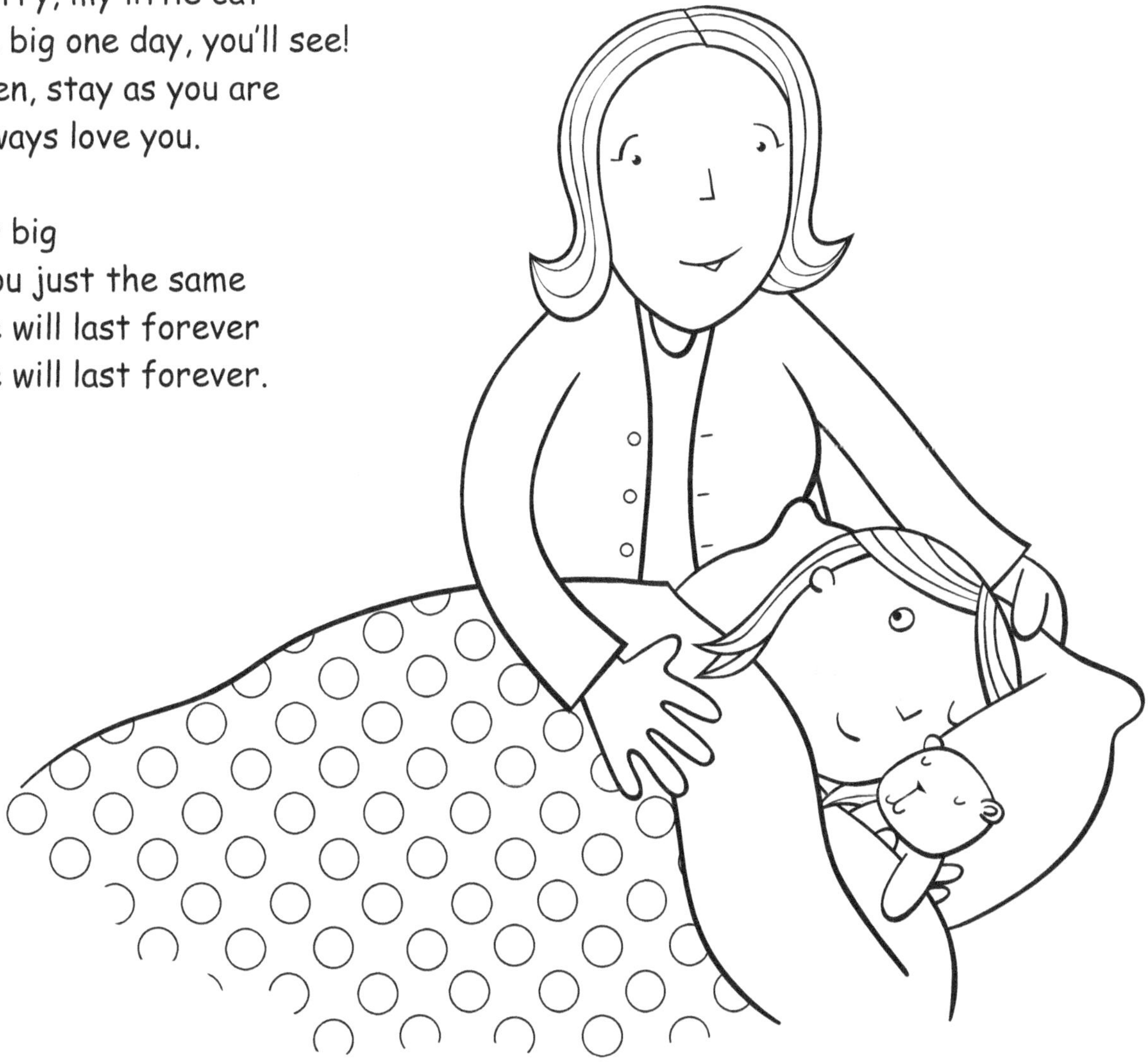

Nom :_____ 10A

10. Petit enfant

en/an

1. Trace the graphemes below and then practise writing them yourself. Say the phoneme out loud as you write it.

en   en

an   an

2. Trace each word below and then practise writing it yourself. Say the word out loud as you write it.

enfant

maman

grand

3. Colour in the picture below if you can read this sentence to a teacher or your partner. Watch out for silent letters in grey.

Le petit **enfan**t aime sa **man**man.

48   21 Fun Songs to Teach French Phonics, 2nd edn
© Brilliant Publications Limited

Nom :_____ 10B

10. Petit enfant

Top tip!
'em' and 'am' also make this phonic sound: décembre, champagne.

en/an

1. Trace the graphemes below then practise writing them yourself. Say the phoneme out loud as you write it.

en   en

an   an

2. Draw a circle around every **en** grapheme and a square around every **an** grapheme.

en	an	eo	ap	an	ai	an	en	ag	en	an
on	an	om	en	an	ai	an	eo	en	an	ep
an	og	en	ag	eo	om	en	ep	an	op	en

How many circles did you draw? ☐   How many squares did you draw? ☐

3. Practise saying the phrases below. Get your partner or teacher to check your pronunciation and colour in the pictures when you are confident you can say all the words correctly.

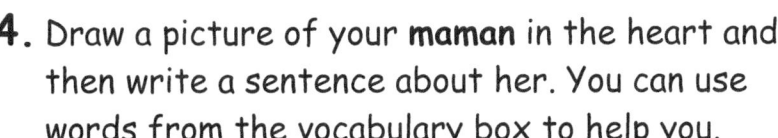
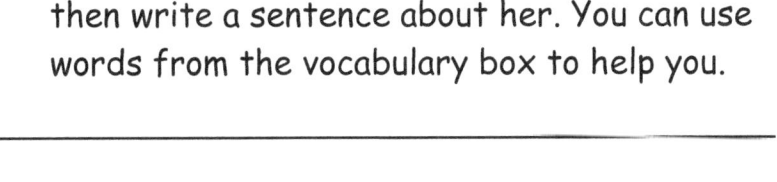

Peti
Petit enfan
Petit enfan aime
Petit enfan aime sa
Petit enfan aime sa maman

Petite
Petite maman
Petite maman aime
Petite maman aime son
Petite maman aime son enfan

4. Draw a picture of your **maman** in the heart and then write a sentence about her. You can use words from the vocabulary box to help you.

_____
_____
_____

Vocabulary
Ma maman est   *My mum is*
gentille   *kind*   fantastique   *fantastic*
marrante   *funny*   élégante   *elegant*

21 Fun Songs to Teach French Phonics, 2nd edn
© Brilliant Publications Limited

11. François le serpent

 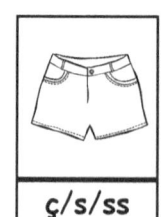

ç/s/ss

François le serpent n'est pas, n'est pas très content !
Il veut faire comme les garçons
Et s'habiller en caleçon
Mais comme il n'a pas de jambes
Chaque fois qu'il essaye, le caleçon tombe, tombe, tombe, tombe !

Sssssssss serpent !

François le serpent, n'est pas, n'est pas très content !
Il veut faire comme les garçons
Et s'habiller en caleçon
Mais comme il n'a pas de jambes
Chaque fois qu'il essaye, le caleçon tombe, tombe, tombe, tombe !

Sssssssss serpent !

11. Francis the snake

ç/s/ss

Francis the snake isn't, isn't very happy!
He wants to be like other boys
And dress himself in boxer shorts
But since he doesn't have any legs
Every time he tries, the boxer shorts fall down, down, down, down!

Sssssssss snake!

Francis the snake isn't, isn't very happy!
He wants to be like other boys
And dress himself in boxer shorts
But since he doesn't have any legs
Every time he tries, the boxer shorts fall down, down, down, down!

Sssssssss snake!

Nom : _____ 11A

11. François le serpent

ç/s/ss

1. Trace the grapheme below and then practise writing it yourself. Pay special attention to the cedilla accent underneath the letter ç. Say the phoneme out loud as you write it.

ç   ç   ç   ç

2. Trace each word below and then practise writing it yourself. Say the word out loud as you write it.

François

caleçon

garçon

3. Colour in the picture below if you can read this sentence to a teacher or your partner. Watch out for silent letters in grey.

Le caleçon de François le serpent tombe !

Nom : _____ 11B

11. François le serpent

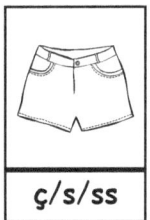

ç/s/ss

1. Trace the grapheme below and then practise writing it yourself. Pay special attention to the cedilla accent underneath the letter **c**. Say the phoneme out loud as you write it.

2. Colour in the snakes below that contain the grapheme **ç** (with a cedilla accent).

3. Unscramble the letters below to make the French words for each of the images.

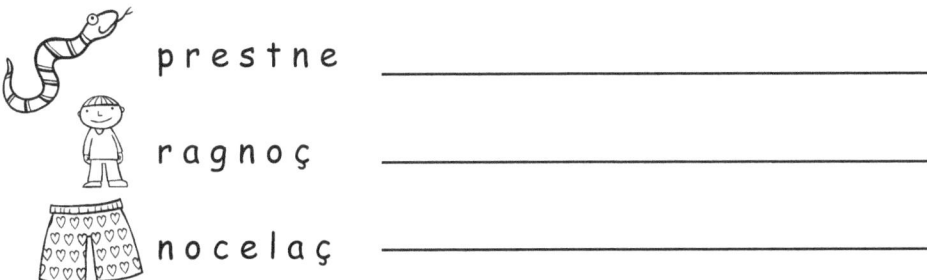

p r e s t n e   _____

r a g n o ç   _____

n o c e l a ç   _____

4. Dress up François using items of clothing and accessories from the vocabulary box. Label your picture.

Vocabulary	
un chapeau	a hat
une écharpe	a scarf
une jupe	skirt
un noeud papillon	a bow tie
un pyjama	pyjamas
une robe	a dress
un sac à main	a handbag
des chaussettes	socks
des chaussures	shoes

5. The French verb for 'to wear' is **porter**. Finish off the sentence below about what François is wearing. The French word for 'and' is '**et**'.

François porte _____

_____

21 Fun Songs to Teach French Phonics, 2nd edn
© Brilliant Publications Limited

12. Gaston le gorille

Tracks
12 & 33

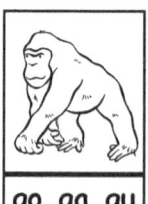

go, ga, gu

Gaston le gorille aime jouer de la guitare
Il n'est jamais fatigué, c'est un vrai fêtard !
Il joue pour ses amis tous les samedis soir
Avec ses godasses dorées, c'est une superstar !

G, g, g, g, g, Gaston ! G, g, g, g, g, gorille ! G, g, g, g, g, guitare !

Gaston le gorille aime jouer de la guitare
Il n'est jamais fatigué, c'est un vrai fêtard !
Il joue pour ses amis tous les samedis soir
Avec ses godasses dorées, c'est une superstar !

G, g, g, g, g, Gaston ! G, g, g, g, g, gorille ! G, g, g, g, g, guitare !

C'est une vraie superstar, oui !

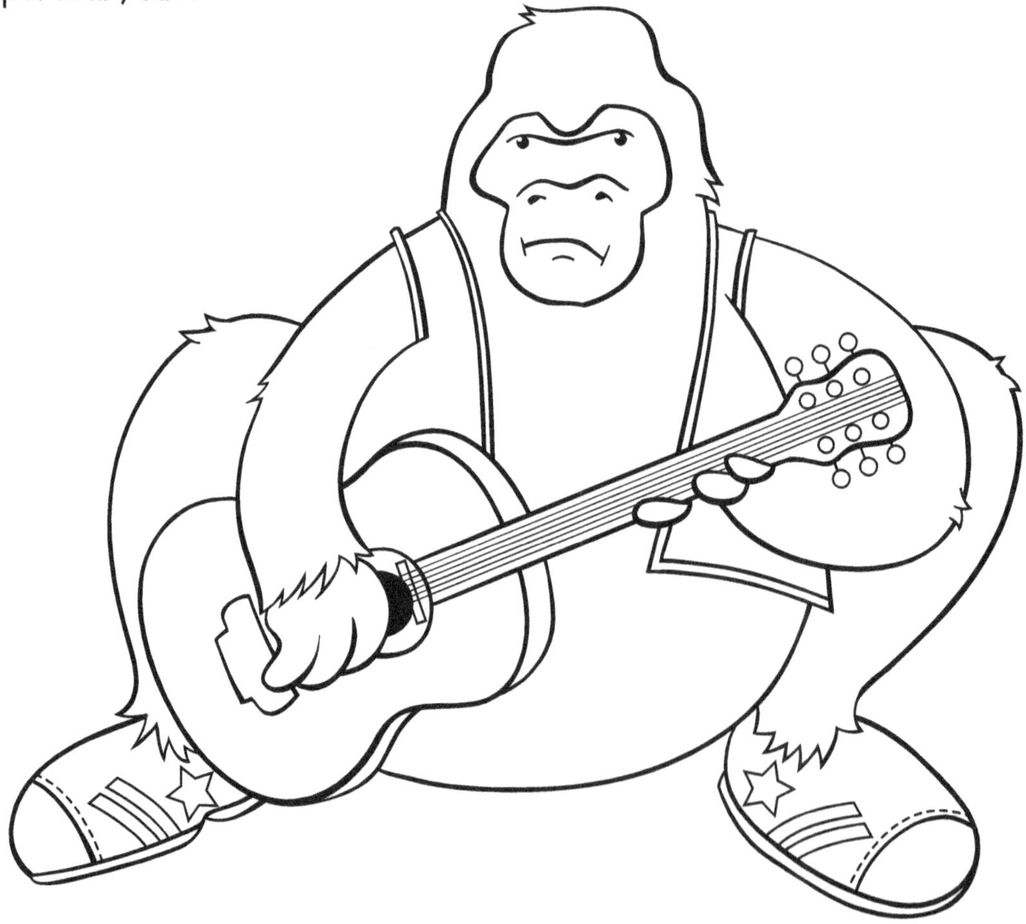

12. Gaston the gorilla

go, ga, gu

Gaston the gorilla likes playing the guitar
He is never tired, he's a real party animal!
He plays for his friends every Saturday evening,
With his gold shoes, he's a superstar!

G, g, g, g, g, Gaston! G,g, g, g, g, gorilla! G, g, g, g, g, guitar!

Gaston the gorilla likes playing the guitar
He is never tired, he's a real party animal!
He plays for his friends every Saturday evening,
With his gold shoes, he's a superstar!

G, g, g, g, g, Gaston! G,g, g, g, g, gorilla! G, g, g, g, g, guitar!

He's a real superstar, yeah!

Nom : _____ 12A

12. Gaston le gorille

go, ga, gu

1. Trace the graphemes below and then practise writing them yourself. Say the phoneme out loud as you write it.

ga   ga   ga

go   go   go

gu   gu   gu

2. Trace each word below and then practise writing it yourself. Say the word out loud as you write it.

Gaston

gorille

guitare

3. Colour in the picture below if you can read this sentence to a teacher or your partner. Watch out for silent letters in grey.

Gaston le gorille porte des godasses dorées pour jouer de la guitare.

56   21 Fun Songs to Teach French Phonics, 2nd edn
© Brilliant Publications Limited

Nom : _____ 12B

12. Gaston le gorille

go, ga, gu

1. Trace the graphemes below and then practise writing them yourself. Say the phoneme out loud as you write it.

ga   ga   ga

go   go   go

gu   gu   gu

2. Circle and shade the words below that contain the graphemes **ga**, **go** and **gu**.

garçon	géographie	géant
guerre		goûter
gomme		jaune
girafe		gagner

3. Draw lines to match up the images with the words.

goûter

guitare

godasse

gorille

4. Draw a picture of **Gaston le gorille**.

5. Practise saying out loud: **Gaston le gorille aime jouer de la guitare**. Ask your teacher or a partner to listen to you and then put a tick in the box when you are confident you can say all the words correctly. ☐

Top tip!
In French, the letter 'g' before 'e', 'i' and 'y' is sounded like the 'j' in the word 'bonjour'. See pages 58–61.

 genou    girafe    gymnastique

21 Fun Songs to Teach French Phonics, 2nd edn
© Brilliant Publications Limited

13. Gigi et Georges

gi, ge, gé

Gigi la girafe et Georges le rouge-gorge
Sont de très bons amis,
Gigi est aussi grande qu'une géante
Et Georges est tout petit.

Gigi et Georges, Gigi et Georges
Gigi et Georges sont amis.

Un jour Georges demande à Gigi :
Pourquoi ton cou est-il si long ?
Gigi réfléchit et répond :
Car mes pieds ne sentent pas très bon !

Gigi et Georges, Gigi et Georges
Gigi et Georges sont amis.

Georges fait une pause et puis il dit :
Il n'y a pas de soucis
À ma hauteur, j'adore l'odeur
Tes pieds sentent bon les fleurs !

Gigi et Georges, Gigi et Georges
Gigi et Georges sont amis.

Gigi et Georges, Gigi et Georges
Gigi et Georges sont amis.

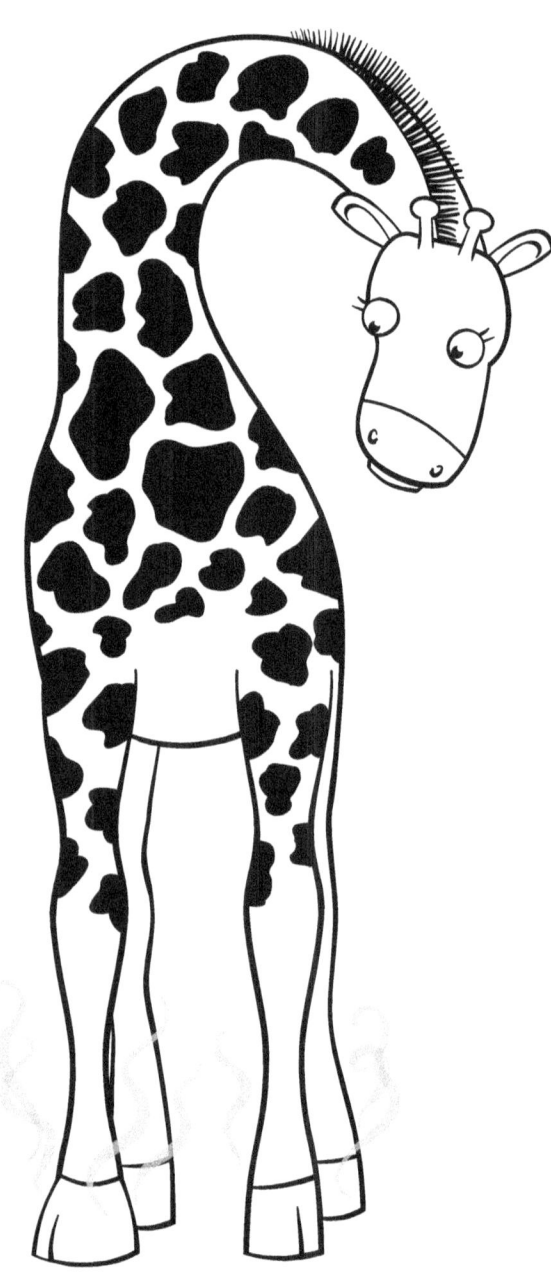

13. Gigi and George

gi, ge, gé

Gigi the giraffe and George the robin
Are very good friends,
Gigi is as tall as a giant
And George is teeny-tiny.

Gigi and George, Gigi and George
Gigi and George are good friends.

One day George asks Gigi:
Why is your neck so long?
Gigi thinks about it and replies:
Because my feet don't smell very nice!

Gigi and George, Gigi and George
Gigi and George are good friends.

George pauses and then he says:
Don't worry about it
From where I'm standing, I love the odour,
Your feet smell like flowers to me!

Gigi and George, Gigi and George
Gigi and George are good friends

Gigi and George, Gigi and George
Gigi and George are good friends

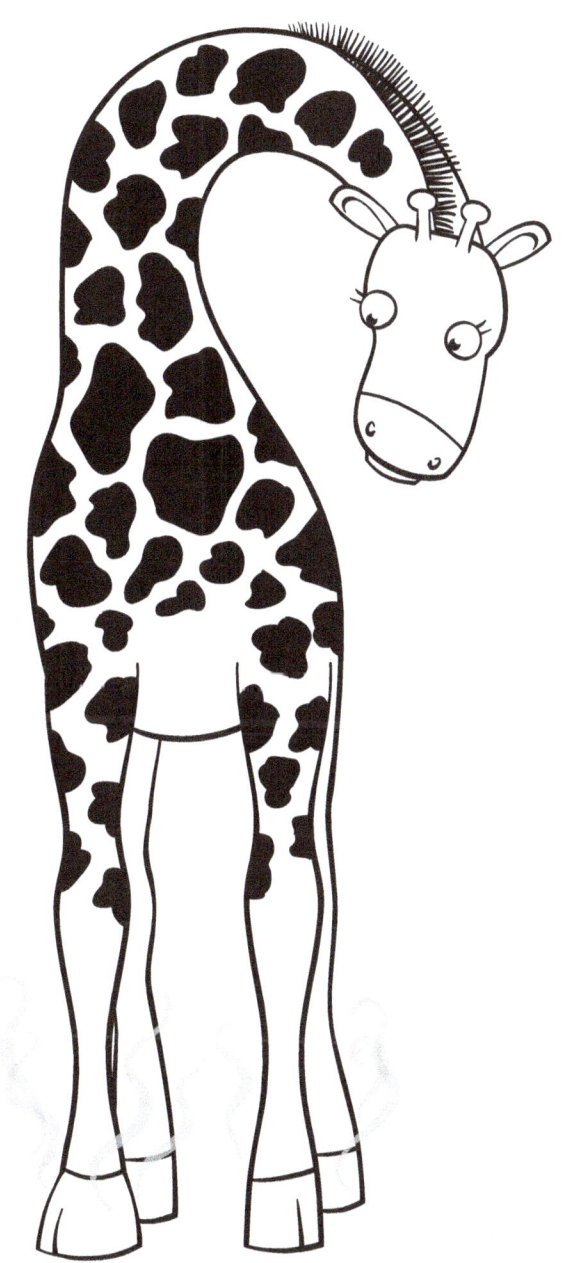

Nom : _____ 13A

13. Gigi et Georges

gi, ge, gé

1. Trace the graphemes below and then practise writing them yourself. Say the phoneme out loud as you write it.

gi gi gi gi

ge ge ge ge

2. Trace each word below and then practise writing it yourself. Say the word out loud as you write it.

 giraffe

 rouge-gorge

 géant

3. Read the sentence below to a teacher or your partner then draw a picture to illustrate it. Watch out for silent letters in grey.

Gigi la girafe et Georges le rouge-gorge sont amis.

Nom : _____ 13B

13. Gigi et Georges

gi, ge, gé

1. Trace the graphemes below and then practise writing them yourself. Say the phoneme out loud as you write it.

2. Draw lines to match up the words on the left with their opposites on the right. You may need to use a dictionary to help you.

grand	vide
froid	vieux
rapide	petit
jeune	chaud
plein	lent

3. Draw a picture of your best friend. Then, using the vocabulary box, write a sentence about why you like him/her.

Vocabulary

J'aime	I like
mon copain	my friend (boy)
ma copine	my friend (girl)
parce qu'il	because he
parce qu'elle	because she
est	is
gentil / gentille	kind (boy/girl)
marrant / marrante	funny (boy/girl)
intelligent / intelligente	clever (boy/girl)
intéressant / intéressante	interesting (boy/girl)

Top tip!
Before the letters 'a', 'o' and 'u', the letter 'g' is pronounced 'hard' like in the English word 'gate'.
　　gagner (*to win*)
　　gomme (*rubber*)
　　guerre (*war*)
See pages 54–57.

_____

_____

_____

14. Chloé et Barnabé

La petite fée Chloé et son ami Barnabé, l'éléphant, l'éléphant,
Ils ne veulent pas aller à l'école en vélo, c'est trop lent, c'est trop lent.
Ils préféreraient y aller en fusée, c'est plus marrant, c'est plus marrant,
Mais comme il y a du vent, ils décident d'y aller en marchant.

La petite fée Chloé et son ami Barnabé, l'éléphant, l'éléphant,
Ils ne veulent pas aller à l'école en vélo, c'est trop lent, c'est trop lent.
Ils préféreraient y aller en fusée, c'est plus marrant, c'est plus marrant,
Mais comme il y a du vent, ils décident d'y aller en sautant.

La petite fée Chloé et son ami Barnabé, l'éléphant, l'éléphant,
Ils ne veulent pas aller à l'école en vélo, c'est trop lent, c'est trop lent.
Ils préféreraient y aller en fusée, c'est plus marrant, c'est plus marrant,
Mais comme il y a du vent, ils décident d'y aller en dansant.

14. Chloe and Barnaby

é/er

Chloe, the little fairy, and her friend Barnaby the elephant, the elephant,
Don't want to go to school by bike, it's too long, it's too long.
They would prefer to go by rocket, that's more fun, that's more fun,
But since it's windy, they decide to walk there instead.

Chloe, the little fairy, and her friend Barnaby the elephant, the elephant
Don't want to go to school by bike, it's too long, it's too long.
They would prefer to go by rocket, that's more fun, that's more fun,
But since it's windy, they decide to jump there instead.

Chloe, the little fairy, and her friend Barnaby the elephant, the elephant
Don't want to go to school by bike, it's too long, it's too long.
They would prefer to go by rocket, that's more fun, that's more fun,
But since it's windy, they decide to dance there instead.

Nom : _____ 14A

14. Chloé et Barnabé

é/er

1. Trace the graphemes below and then practise writing them yourself. Pay special attention to the acute accent on é. Say the phoneme out loud as you write it.

é é é é

er er er er

2. Trace each word below and then practise writing it yourself. Say the word out loud as you write it.

 fée

  éléphant

 fusée

3. Colour in the picture below if you can read this sentence to your teacher or your partner. Watch out for silent letters in grey.

Je voudrais aller
à l'école en fusée
avec Chloé
et Barnabé !

Nom :_____ 14B

14. Chloé et Barnabé

é/er

1. Trace the graphemes below and then practise writing them yourself. Pay special attention to the acute accent on the letter **é**. Say the phoneme out loud as you write it.

é é é é

er er er er

2. Circle all the words that contain the grapheme **é**.

ami éléphant vent école fée lent fusée marrant vélo petite

How many words did you circle? ☐

3. Practise saying the following French verbs, paying careful attention to the **er** phonic sound at the end. Ask your partner or teacher to listen to your pronunciation and colour in each star when you are confident you can say the verb correctly.

aller manger écouter regarder parler marcher

4. Which methods of transport would you like to take to go to school? Draw a picture and complete the sentence, using the vocabulary box to help you.

Je voudrais aller à l'école _____

_____

_____

Vocabulary
en voiture 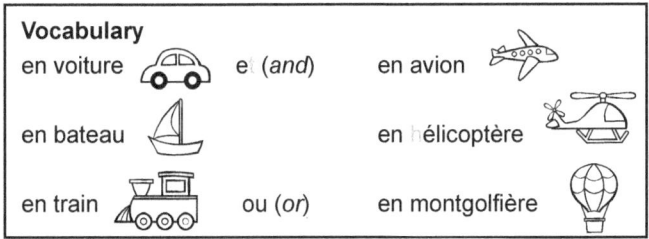 et (and) en avion
en bateau en hélicoptère
en train ou (or) en montgolfière

Top tip!
You can also make the same phonic sound using the spelling **ez**: le n**ez** (the nose), tais**ez**-vous! (be quiet!) Note that the word '**et**' (and) also makes this phonic sound, although the letter string '**et**' in other words (poul**et**, for example) does not.

15. Du lundi au dimanche

Voici les jours de la semaine !

Lundi, je reste au lit
Mardi, je mange du riz
Mercredi, je fais du ski
Jeudi, je jongle avec des fruits
Oui, oui, oui, oui !
Vendredi, je dis merci
Samedi, je vois mes amis

Mais le dimanche est différent
Car le « di » est placé à l'avant
Dimanche, dimanche, dimanche !

Et puis c'est lundi et tout recommence !

Lundi, je reste au lit
Mardi, je mange du riz
Mercredi, je fais du ski
Jeudi, je jongle avec des fruits
Oui, oui, oui, oui !
Vendredi, je dis merci
Samedi, je vois mes amis

Mais le dimanche est différent
Car le « di » est placé à l'avant
Dimanche, dimanche, dimanche !

Et puis c'est lundi et tout recommence !

15. From Monday to Sunday

Here are the days of the week!

Monday, I stay in bed
Tuesday, I eat rice
Wednesday, I go skiing
Thursday, I juggle with some fruit
Yeah, yeah, yeah, yeah!
Friday, I say thank you
Saturday, I see my friends

But Sunday is different
Because the 'di' is placed at the front
Sunday, Sunday, Sunday!

And then it's Monday and it starts all over again!

Monday, I stay in bed
Tuesday, I eat rice
Wednesday, I go skiing
Thursday, I juggle with some fruit
Yeah, yeah, yeah, yeah!
Friday, I say thank you
Saturday, I see my friends

But Sunday is different
Because the 'di' is placed at the front
Sunday, Sunday, Sunday!

And then it's Monday and it starts all over again!

Nom : _____ 15A

15. Du lundi au dimanche

i

1. Trace the grapheme below and then practise writing it yourself. Say the phoneme out loud as you write it.

i i i i i

2. Trace each word below and then practise writing it yourself. Say the word out loud as you write it.

lit

ski

riz

3. Colour in the picture below if you can read these sentences to a teacher or your partner. Watch out for silent letters in grey.

Youpi ! C'est Samedi !
Je peux rester au lit !

Nom : _____ 15B

15. Du lundi au dimanche

Top tip!
'y' also makes this phonic sound: gymnastique, stylo.

i

1. Trace the grapheme below then practise writing it yourself. Say the phoneme out loud as you write it.

2. Write the French days of the week in the correct order in box A. Use box B to help you.

A
```
_ _ _ _ d i
_ _ _ _ d i
_ _ _ _ _ _ _ d i
_ _ _ _ d i
_ _ _ _ _ _ _ d i
_ _ _ _ _ d i
d i _ _ _ _ _ _ _
```

B
```
mercre
vendre
mar
lun
manche
jeu
same
```

3. Fill in the gaps in each sentence below using the words in the box to help you.

a) Lundi, je reste au _____ .

b) Mardi, je _____ du riz.

c) Mercredi, je fais du _____ .

d) Jeudi, je jongle avec des _____ .

e) Vendredi, je dis _____ .

f) Samedi, je _____ mes amis.

```
merci
ski
fruits
mange
vois
lit
```

4. Answer the following question in French: **qu'est-ce que tu fais le dimanche ?** (What do you do on Sundays?) Start your answer with: **Le dimanche, je ….**

_____

_____

Top tip!
Unlike in English, the days of the week in French **do not have capital letters** (unless they are at the start of a sentence).

16. Papy, raconte-moi une histoire !

Tracks 16 & 37

oi

Papy, raconte-moi une histoire !
La nuit, il fait froid et j'ai peur du noir !
Je crois qu'il y a un monstre dans le couloir !
Papy, raconte-moi une histoire !

Une histoire de dragons et de rois
Une histoire de gros loup dans le bois
Une histoire de sheriff qui fait la loi
Une histoire qui raconte n'importe quoi !

Papy, raconte-moi une histoire !
La nuit, il fait froid et j'ai peur du noir !
Je crois qu'il y a un monstre dans le couloir !
Papy, raconte-moi une histoire !

Mon petit coeur, maintenant c'est l'heure
De hisser la grand-voile, à la belle étoile
Laisse-toi bercer et fais dodo
Aux pays des réglisses et chamallows.

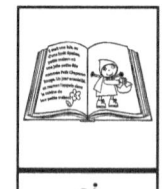

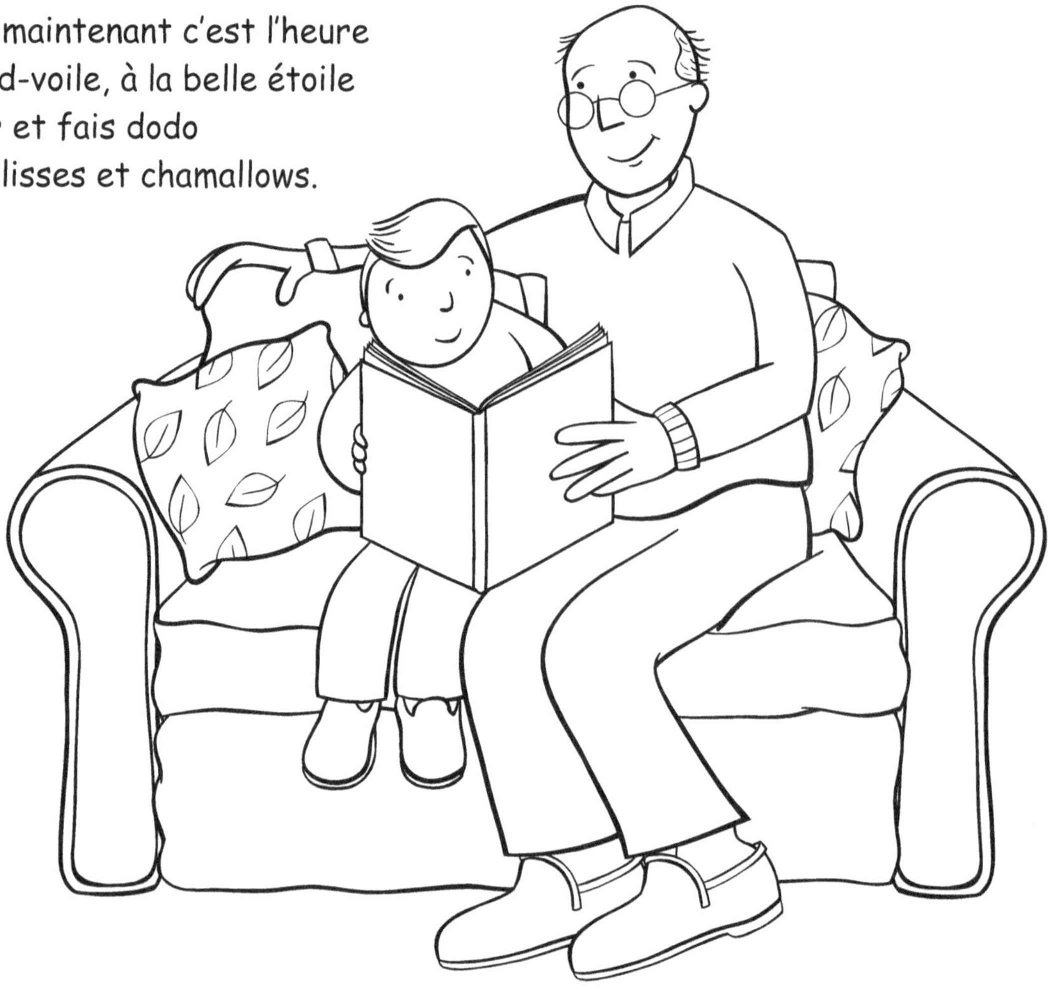

16. Grandpa, tell me a story!

oi

Grandpa, tell me a story!
At night, it's cold and I'm afraid of the dark.
I think there's a monster in the hallway!
Grandpa, tell me a story!

A story of dragons and kings
A story of a big wolf in the woods
A story of a sheriff laying down the law
A story about anything at all!

Grandpa, tell me a story!
At night, it's cold and I'm afraid of the dark.
I think there's a monster in the hallway!
Grandpa, tell me a story!

My little sweetheart, now it's time
To set sail under the stars
Let yourself be rocked and go to sleep
In the land of liquorice and marshmallows.

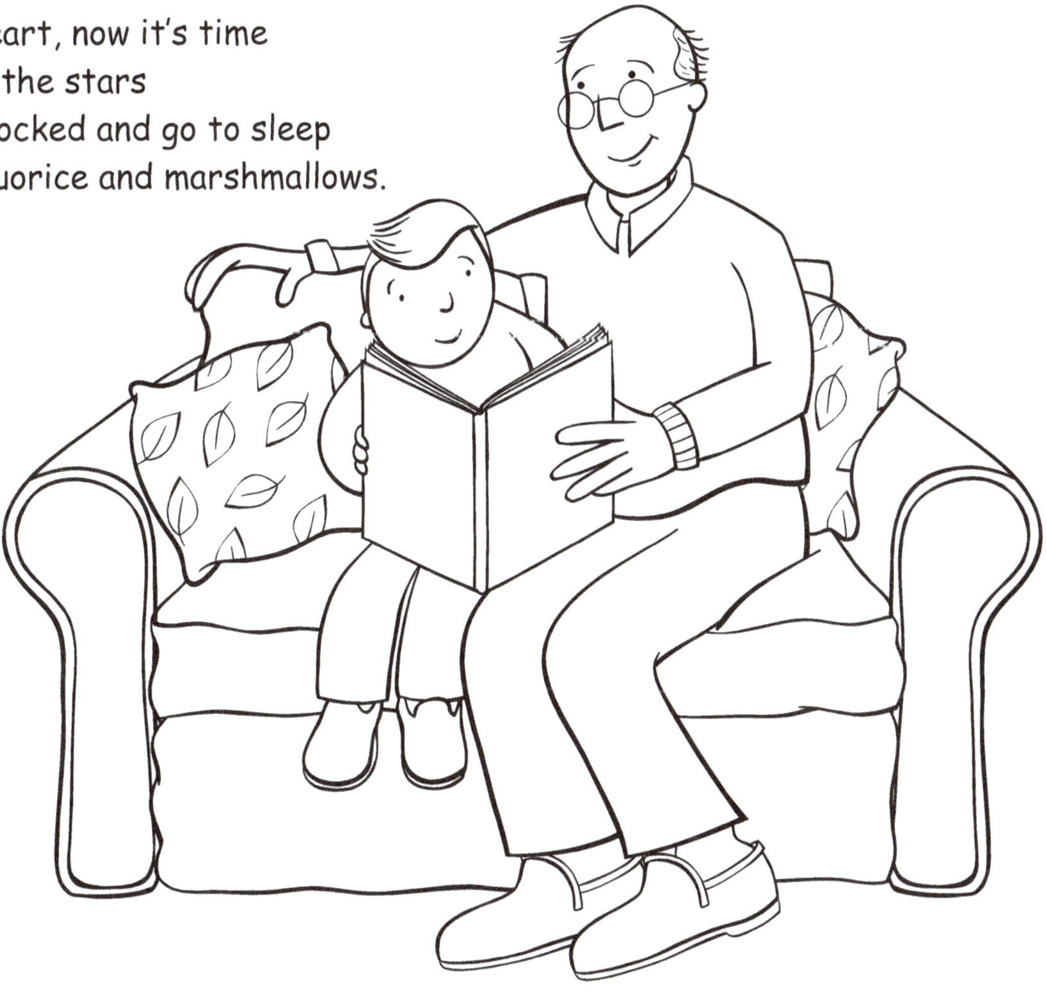

Nom : _____ 16A

16. Papy, raconte-moi une histoire !

1. Trace the grapheme below and then practise writing it yourself. Say the phoneme out loud as you write it.

oi   oi   oi

2. Trace each word below and then practise writing it yourself. Say the word out loud as you write it.

   histoire

   roi

   étoile

3. Read the sentence below to a teacher or your partner then draw a picture to illustrate it. Watch out for silent letters in grey.

Le roi mange du poisson froid avec des petits pois !

Nom :_____ 16B

16. Papy, raconte-moi une histoire !

oi

1. Trace the grapheme below and then practise writing it yourself. Say the phoneme out loud as you write it.

oi   oi   oi   oi

2. Colour in the dragons below that contain the grapheme **oi**.

histoire froid monstre noir loup moi

3. Draw pictures to illustrate the following phrases:

Une histoire de dragons et de rois

Une histoire de gros loup dans le bois

Papy, raconte-moi une histoire

4. Complete the crossword below by translating the clues into French.

Across
2 star

4 black

6 hallway

Down
1 story

3 cold

5 king

21 Fun Songs to Teach French Phonics, 2nd edn
© Brilliant Publications Limited
73

17. Une glace à la vanille

ille

J'aime aller à la plage avec ma famille
J'aime jouer avec tous les garçons et les filles
J'aime sentir sur ma peau le soleil qui brille
Et j'adore manger une glace à la vanille !

Avec une sauce au caramel ! Avec une sauce au caramel !
Avec une sauce au caramel ! Avec une sauce au caramel !

J'aime aller à la plage avec ma famille
J'aime jouer avec tous les garçons et les filles
J'aime sentir sur ma peau le soleil qui brille
Et j'adore manger une glace à la vanille !

Avec une sauce au chocolat ! Avec une sauce au chocolat !
Avec une sauce au chocolat ! Avec une sauce au chocolat !

17. Vanilla ice cream

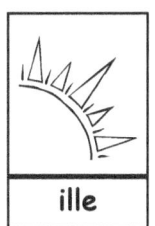
ille

I like going to the beach with my family
I like playing with all the boys and girls
I like feeling the sun shining on my skin
And I love eating vanilla ice cream!

With caramel sauce! With caramel sauce!
With caramel sauce! With caramel sauce!

I like going to the beach with my family
I like playing with all the boys and girls
I like feeling the sun shining on my skin
And I love eating vanilla ice cream!

With chocolate sauce! With chocolate sauce!
With chocolate sauce! With chocolate sauce!

Nom : _____   17A

17. Une glace à la vanille

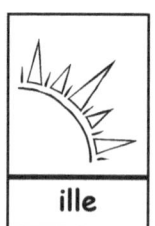

1. Trace the grapheme below and then practise writing it yourself. Say the phoneme out loud as you write it.

2. Trace each word below and then practise writing it yourself. Say the word out loud as you write it.

3. Colour in the picture below if you can read this sentence to a teacher or your partner. Watch out for silent letters in grey.

Toutes les **fille**s dans ma fam**ille** mangent des glaces à la van**ille** !

Nom :_____ 17B

17. Une glace à la vanille

ille

1. Trace the grapheme below and then practise writing it yourself. Say the phoneme out loud as you write it.

ille   ille   ille

2. Circle the **four** words below that contain the grapheme **ille**.

fille   bulle   bille   utile   gorille   sourcils   cheville   milieu   aller

3. Use the images to help you unscramble the words below that contain the grapheme **ille**. You may need a dictionary to help you.

   i h n e l c l e   _____

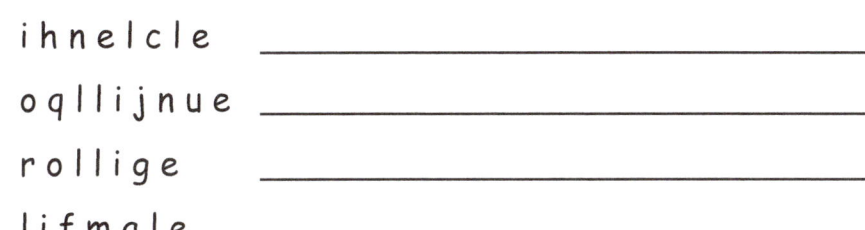   o q l l i j n u e   _____

r o l l i g e   _____

l i f m a l e   _____

4. Colour in the ice creams below according to the description of their flavours.

une glace à la menthe   une glace au citron   une glace à la fraise   une glace au chocolat

5. Using words from the song and a dictionary to help you, draw and label in French a picture of you and your **famille à la plage**.

18. Le rap du hérisson

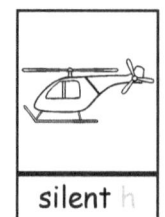

silent h

Hervé le hérisson
A mangé trop de bonbons.
Hic hic hic ! Il a le hoquet !
À l'hôpital ! Il faut le soigner !
On y va en hélicoptère
Aïe, aïe, aïe ! Pauvre pépère !

Hector le hippo
A mangé trop de chamallows.
Hic hic hic ! Il a le hoquet !
À l'hôpital ! Il faut le soigner !
On y va en hélicoptère
Aïe, aïe, aïe ! Pauvre pépère !

Harry le hamster
A mangé trop de hamburgers.
Hic hic hic ! Il a le hoquet !
À l'hôpital ! Il faut le soigner !
On y va en hélicoptère
Aïe, aïe, aïe ! Pauvre pépère !

Quelle est la morale de cette histoire ?
Écoute-moi bien et tu vas savoir !
Si tu veux rester en bonne santé
Il faut manger équilibré !
Si tu as compris, chante avec moi :
Hip, hip, hip hoorah !

18. The hedgehog rap

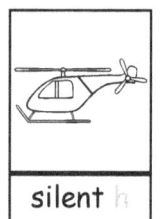
silent h

Harvey the hedgehog
Has eaten too many sweets
Hic hic hic! He's got the hiccups!
To hospital! He needs to be treated!
Let's go by helicopter
Ouch, ouch, ouch! Poor thing!

Hector the hippo
Has eaten too many marshmallows
Hic hic hic! He's got the hiccups!
To hospital! He needs to be treated!
Let's go by helicopter
Ouch, ouch, ouch! Poor thing!

Harry the hamster
Has eaten too many hamburgers
Hic hic hic! He's got the hiccups!
To hospital! He needs to be treated!
Let's go by helicopter
Ouch, ouch, ouch! Poor thing!

What is the moral of this story?
Listen carefully and you will find out
If you want to stay fit
You need to eat healthily!
If you've got it, sing with me:
Hip, hip, hip hooray!

18. Le rap du hérisson

Nom : _____ 18A

Top tip!
The letter h is always silent in French, except in combination with the letter 'c' – **ch**at (see pages 38–41).

silent h

1. Trace each word below and then practise writing it yourself. Say the word out loud as you write it. Remember not to pronounce the letter h at the start of each word.

 hérisson

 hôpital

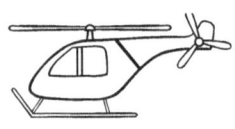 hélicoptère

2. Read the sentence below to a teacher or your partner then draw a picture to illustrate it. Watch out for silent letters in grey.

Hervé le hérisson va à l'hôpital en hélicoptère.

Nom : _____ 18B

18. Le rap du hérisson

Top tip! The letter **h** is always silent in French, except in combination with the letter 'c' – **ch**at (see pages 38–41).

silent h

1. Practise saying the words below, being careful not to pronounce the letter **h** at the start. Colour in the pictures when you are confident you can say the words correctly.

hérisson   hélicoptère   hôpital

2. Make up your own story about a greedy animal! Using the vocabulary box below, choose and shade an option from each of the tables, then draw a picture.

a)

Henri		requin			chocolat
Hugo	le	serpent	à mangé trop de	beignets
Hubert		tigre			frites

b)

	mal au ventre !			en moto
Il a	mal à la tête !	À l'hôpital ! On y va	en voiture
	mal à la gorge !			en avion

3. Write out the two French sentences you created in exercise 2.

a) _____
_____
_____

b) _____
_____
_____

Vocabulary
requin — shark
serpent — snake
tigre — tiger
chocolat — chocolate
beignets — doughnuts
frites — chips
mal au ventre — a tummy ache
mal à la tête — a headache
mal à la gorge — a sore throat
en moto — by bike
en voiture — by car
en avion — by aeroplane

4. Practise saying this tongue-twister. Remember not to pronounce the letter **h** !

Hervé le hérisson a hâte de hiberner cet hiver avec Harry le hamster.

19. Qu'est-ce que … ?

Qu'est-ce que tu fais aujourd'hui ?
Je joue au foot avec mes amis.

Qu'est-ce que tu as fait hier ?
J'ai fait du skate avec mon frère.

Qu'est-ce que tu vas faire demain ?
Je vais promener mon chien.

Que, que, que, que, qu'est-ce que ?
Que, que, que, que, qu'est-ce que ?
Que, que, que, que, qu'est-ce que ?

Que, que, que, que, qu'est-ce que ?
Que, que, que, que, qu'est-ce que ?
Que, que, que, que, qu'est-ce que ?

Qu'est-ce que tu fais aujourd'hui ?
Je fais du ski avec mes amis.

Qu'est-ce que tu as fait hier ?
J'ai cuisiné avec ma mère.

Qu'est-ce que tu vas faire demain ?
Je vais acheter du pain.

Que, que, que, que, qu'est-ce que ?
Que, que, que, que, qu'est-ce que ?
Que, que, que, que, qu'est-ce que ?

Que, que, que, que, qu'est-ce que ?
Que, que, que, que, qu'est-ce que ?
Que, que, que, que, qu'est-ce que ?

Qu'est-ce que ?

19. What...?

What are you doing today?
I'm playing football with my friends.

What did you do yesterday?
I went skateboarding with my brother.

What are you going to do tomorrow?
I'm going to walk my dog.

W – w – w -w what?
W – w – w -w what?
W – w – w -w what?

W – w – w -w what?
W – w – w -w what?
W – w – w -w what?

What are you doing today?
I'm going skiing with my friends.

What did you do yesterday?
I cooked with my mum.

What are you going to do tomorrow?
I am going to buy some bread.

W – w – w -w what?
W – w – w -w what?
W – w – w -w what?

W – w – w -w what?
W – w – w -w what?
W – w – w -w what?

What?

Nom : _____ 19A

19. Qu'est-ce que ... ?

1. Trace the grapheme below and then practise writing it yourself. Say the phoneme out loud as you write it.

2. Trace each word below and then practise writing it yourself. Say the word out loud as you write it.

3. Read the sentence below to a teacher or your partner then draw a picture to illustrate your ideal birthday party. Watch out for silent letters in grey.

Qu'est-ce que tu fais pour ton anniversaire ? Qui vient à ta fête ?

Nom : _____ 19B

19. Qu'est-ce que ... ?

1. Trace the grapheme below and then practise writing it yourself. Say the phoneme out loud as you write it.

   qu   qu   qu

2. Draw lines to match up the French question words on the left with their English translations on the right. You may need to use a dictionary to help you.

Qui	How
Quand	Why
Quel	How many
Où	Is it that (do you)
Comment	Who
Est-ce que	When
Combien	What is it that (what do you)
Pourquoi	Which
Qu'est-ce que	Where

3. Draw pictures to illustrate the phrases in the boxes below:

Aujourd'hui	Hier	Demain
Je joue au foot avec mes amis.	**J'ai fait** du skate avec mon frère.	**Je vais** promener mon chien.

4. Using the sentence structures in exercise 3 above, write three sentences in French about what you are doing today, what you did yesterday and what you are going to do tomorrow.

   Aujourd'hui, je joue _____

   Hier, j'ai fait _____

   Demain, je vais _____

21 Fun Songs to Teach French Phonics, 2nd edn
© Brilliant Publications Limited

20. Trois oiseaux

s sounds like z

Il y a trois oiseaux dans mon jardin
Un mange les fraises, un autre les raisins
Le troisième préfère les cerises
Et pour dire merci, il me fait la bise !

Chantez, petits oiseaux
Volez, vous êtes si beaux !
Prenez-moi sous vos ailes
Emmenez-moi dans le ciel.

Il y a trois oiseaux dans mon jardin
Un mange les fraises, un autre les raisins
Le troisième préfère les cerises
Et pour dire merci, il me fait la bise !

Chantez, petits oiseaux !
Volez, vous êtes si beaux !
Prenez-moi sous vos ailes
Emmenez-moi dans le ciel.

20. Three birds

s sounds like z

There are three birds in my garden
One eats strawberries, another eats grapes
The third prefers cherries
And to say thank you, he kisses me on the cheek!

Sing, little birds!
Fly, you are so beautiful!
Take me underneath your wings
Carry me to the sky.

There are three birds in my garden
One eats strawberries, another eats grapes
The third prefers cherries
And to say thank you, he kisses me on the cheek!

Sing, little birds!
Fly, you are so beautiful!
Take me underneath your wings
Carry me to the sky.

Nom : _____ 20A

20. Trois oiseaux

1. Trace each word below and then practise writing it yourself. Say the word out loud as you write it.

 fraises

 raisins

 cerises

2. Colour in the picture below if you can read this sentence to a teacher or your partner. Watch out for silent letters in grey.

Les oiseaux mangent les fraises, les cerises et les raisins dans mon jardin.

Nom :_____ 20B

20. Trois oiseaux

s sounds like z

1. In French, the letter **s** sounds like a **z** when it is between two vowels within a word. For example: oi<u>s</u>eau, frai<u>s</u>e, ceri<u>s</u>e, rai<u>s</u>in.

Practise saying the word **oiseau**, paying careful attention to the **z** sound in the middle. Get your partner or teacher to check your pronunciation and colour in a bird each time you say **oiseau** correctly.

2. An **s** at the end of a word is usually silent. For example: troi~~s~~. However, it is sounded like a **z** when it is followed by a vowel or silent **h** at the start of the next word. This is called a liaison. For example:

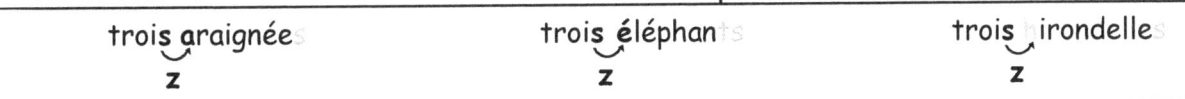

| trois araignées | trois éléphants | trois hirondelles |
| z | z | z |

Practise saying the phrase **trois oiseaux**, paying careful attention to the two **z** sounds. Get your partner or teacher to check your pronunciation and colour in a group of three birds each time you say **trois oiseaux** correctly.

3. Read the description of a garden then draw a picture of it in the box. **Dans mon jardin, il y a trois arbres et beaucoup de fleurs. Il y a un escargot, deux araignées et trois oiseaux. Il y a aussi quatre fraises, cinq raisins et six cerises.**

21 Fun Songs to Teach French Phonics, 2nd edn
© Brilliant Publications Limited

21. Le petit canard Coin-coin

oin

Le petit canard Coin-coin
Un jour est parti trop loin
Il s'est perdu dans le foin
Il a besoin d'un coup de main.

Allez, Coin-coin
Ne vas pas trop loin
Allez, Coin-coin
Viens voir tes copains
Allez Coin-coin, Coin-coin.

Le petit canard Coin-coin,
Un jour est parti trop loin
Il s'est perdu dans le foin
Il a besoin d'un coup de main.

Allez, Coin-coin
Ne vas pas trop loin
Allez, Coin-coin
Viens voir tes copains
C'est l'heure de prendre ton bain.

Coin-coin !

21. Quack-quack the litte duck

oin

Quack-quack the little duck
Went too far one day
He got lost in the hay
He needs a helping hand.

Come on, Quack-quack
Don't go too far
Come on, Quack-quack
Come and see your friends
Come on Quack-quack, Quack-quack.

Quack-quack the little duck
Went too far one day
He got lost in the hay
He needs a helping hand.

Come on, Quack-quack
Don't go too far
Come on, Quack-quack
Come and see your friends
It's time to take your bath!

Quack-quack!!

Nom : _____ 21A

21. Le petit canard Coin-coin

oin

1. Trace the grapheme below and then practise writing it yourself. Say the phoneme out loud as you write it.

   oin   oin   oin

2. Trace each word below and then practise writing it yourself. Say the word out loud as you write it.

   Coin-coin

   foin

   loin

3. Colour in the picture below if you can read this sentence to a teacher or your partner. Watch out for silent letters in grey.

En allant trop loin, Coin-coin s'est perdu dans le foin !

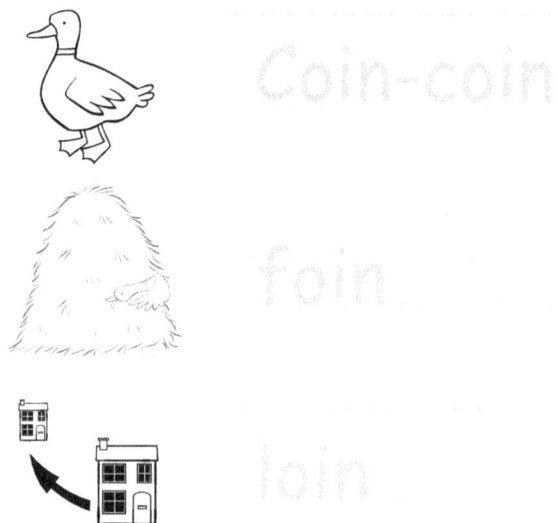

Nom : _____ 21B

21. Le petit canard Coin-coin

oin

1. Trace the grapheme below and then practise writing it yourself. Say the phoneme out loud as you write it.

oin   oin   oin

2. Circle the **four** words below that contain the grapheme **oin**.

poids   loin   fois   coin   grenouille   besoin   témoin   toît

3. Complete the word search below, then translate the words into English. The words can go forwards, backwards, up, down and diagonally.

```
o c v z t c a k o z i h a f t
o b t r y a z r d f d y l m f
k r n j o n q n f m w y x e h
f b l y c a a n e i h c r c o
h u n q e r o k z g q l p g n
m v x i g d x t m t i t e p e
w d e l o m a v t t g u j g w
m w o c w s h m b t z u l x n
n a l j v b e q p d e i d s q
z c h e v a l b e m r e f e i
q n i o f w c z n o h c o c r
p q o t k l s h w i h d s c b
j x t o e v p t g h o v b u t
s y o j x i q z v i a l s q n
b u n e q x j s n k g n p r r
```

canard _____
cheval _____
chien _____
foin _____
loin _____
besoin _____
cochon _____
petit _____
grand _____
ferme _____

4. Colour in the picture below according to the following colour code:
Coin-coin = jaune
foin   = marron
cochon   = rose
chien   = noir
cheval   = gris

21 Fun Songs to Teach French Phonics, 2nd edn
© Brilliant Publications Limited

French phonics progress chart

Key graphemes

Colour in each picture as you learn its phonic sound.

				un
				un

o/eau	ou	gn	u
cachalot	loup	araignée	tortue
on	**ien**	**ch**	**ê/è**
cochon	chien	chat	bête
en/an	**ç/s/ss**	**go/ga/gu**	**gi/ge/gé**
enfant	caleçon	gorille	girafe
é/er	**i**	**oi**	**ille**
éléphant	ski	histoire	brille
silent h	**qu**	**s sounds like z**	**oin**
hélicoptère	qu'est-ce que ?	oiseaux	Coin-coin

Teaching ideas

Here are some ideas for activities and games to support the teaching and learning of **21 Fun Songs to Teach French Phonics**.

Spot the French phonics!
Work as a class, in teams or individually.
Using the lyrics: project the grapheme(s) on to the board. Give groups a printout of the lyrics and then play the song. Whenever students hear the corresponding phoneme, they have to underline the word that it is found in. This can also be done without playing the music, with children reading the lyrics instead.

Using physical gestures: play the song and every time the pupils hear the phoneme, they raise their hand/do the action you have chosen as a class.

1. Il y a quelqu'un ?   page 10
Choose one pupil to be the 'caller' and then split the rest of the class into three groups. The caller says the line « *Allô, allô? Il y a quelqu'un ?* » The other three groups represent the rabbit, horse and bird. They each sing their verse and must come up with their own actions. All pupils can join in with « *Chantez, dansez, tapez trois, deux, un* » etc. Remember to switch the groups around so that every child gets a go at each part.

2. Mon cachalot   page 14
What else might the pupils find in their bucket? Brainstorm some vocabulary using the pupils' ideas and then reinforce the phrase: « d*ans mon seau il y a un/une… .*» The song could then be performed replacing the word « *cachalot* » for one of the pupils' words instead. The concept of gender and the indefinite article could be introduced/reinforced at this point.

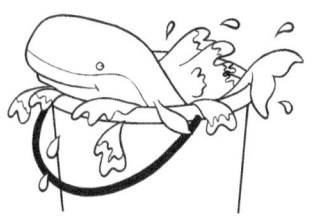

3. Mon petit loup   page 18
Split the class up into pairs. One pupil is the child and the other pupil is the wolf. Can they use the lyrics like a script and act out the story? If you have any very shy or reluctant pupils, they could be the owl and join in with the actions. Ask for volunteers to act out the story to the rest of the class.

4. Une araignée dans ma baignoire   page 22
Art and craft activity: make a spider! You will need 8 pipe cleaners, 1 pompom, 2 googly eyes and some glue. You can use this activity to introduce body parts (*la tête, les yeux, les pattes*, etc).

5. Lulu la tortue   page 26
Can pupils imagine who Lulu may have met on Neptune? Who did she play football with? What did she eat for her picnic? Brainstorm vocabulary on the board and then ask them to draw and label a picture.

6. Le rock 'n' roll du cochon   page 30

Split the class in half. Have one half leading the singing and the other half singing the echoes. Ask for a volunteer to lead on their own and have the rest of the class echo them.

The teacher calls out an animal and the rest of the class have to do the corresponding action, e.g. « *le cochon….mange des bonbons* » (the pig is eating sweets). This could be turned into a game of *Jacques a dit* (Simon says) or you could ask for a pupil to be the teacher and call out the animals. Alternatively, the teacher does an action, e.g. eating sweets, and asks the students to call out which animal the action belongs to. In this case it would be « *le cochon* ».

Can the pupils think of any other animals that could be doing something funny or surprising? Can they draw a picture and label it? Perhaps a new version of the song could be made up using the pupils' ideas.

7. Mon ami Julien   page 34

Ask the pupils to replace the animals in the song with other animals of their choice (*dinosaure, licorne, cochon d'Inde*, etc). Use this song as an opportunity to talk about their pets using the question: « *As-tu un animal ?* » (Do you have an animal?). Pupils can respond with: « *oui, j'ai un/une …* » or « *non, mais j'aimerais un/une …* ».

8. Le chat en chocolat   page 38

Pupils stand in a circle. Whilst singing the song, they have to pass the ball around the circle. (It can be thrown across the circle to make it harder.) If the ball is dropped, then they have to sing the song again from the start. The aim of the game is to get to the end of the song without dropping the ball. Harder than it sounds!

This song can also be used to demonstrate the French vowel sounds: a, e, i, o, u. Each of the five verses concentrates on one vowel sound:
1) *chat, chocolat, rat* (a)
2) *oeufs, heureux* (e)
3) *sourit, ami* (i)
4) *eau, chaud* (o)
5) *disparu, déçu* (u)

9. Il y a une petite bête   page 42

Sit in a circle and use a soft toy to represent the « *bête* ». Whilst singing the song one pupil walks around the circle. When it gets to the chorus (*elle danse, elle chante …*, etc) the child stops and gets the soft toy to act out singing and dancing on the head of the person he or she is stood behind. At the end of the chorus, the child who was sitting under the « *bête* » takes over, walking around the circle until the next chorus, etc. Be warned: pupils will probably also want to act out the line: « *il faudrait pas qu'elle pète !* » (let's hope it doesn't trump!)

10. Petit enfant   page 46

Practise using numbers: ask pupils to measure each other's height, and see if they can tell the rest of the class how tall they are using French numbers, e.g. *un mètre vingt*.

Who is *le/la plus grand(e) dans la classe* (the tallest in the class) and *le/la plus petit(e)* (the smallest)? The phrases « *je suis grand(e), je suis petit(e), je suis de taille moyenne* » (I am tall/short/medium height) could be introduced/reinforced.

Possessive adjectives indicate ownership ('my', 'your', 'his/her', 'our', 'their' in English). Unlike in English, French possessive adjectives refer to the gender of the noun that is owned, not the person who owns it. For example, in English we would say 'his apple' to talk about Hugo's apple. We would say 'her apple' to talk about Suzanne's apple. In French, however, we would say 'sa pomme' for both Hugo and Suzanne, because 'sa' is the feminine version of the possessive adjective that is used because 'pomme' is a feminine word. So 'sa' can mean both 'his' and 'her'. Here are some examples:

Voici Hugo. Je connais **sa** mère.
Here is Hugo. I know **his** mother.
Voici Suzanne. Je connais **sa** mère.
Here is Suzanne. I know **her** mother.

Voici Hugo. Je connais **son** frère.
Here is Hugo. I know **his** brother.
Voici Suzanne. Je connais **son** frère.
Here is Suzanne. I know **her** brother.

In the song Petit Enfant, the gender of the child is not specified, so 'sa maman' could mean 'his mum' or 'her mum'. Up to you and your pupils to decide!

11. François le serpent   page 50
Ask pupils to design and label a pair of boxer shorts (or other items of clothing) for François. This could be a good opportunity to revise clothing, colours and adjective position and agreement. The pupils' designs could be displayed or cut out and hung up on a washing line in the classroom.

12. Gaston le gorille   page 54
Practising musical instruments: ask pupils to change the song lyrics so that Gaston plays other instruments. Reinforce the construction « *jouer de + instrument* »: *je joue de la guitare, je joue de la batterie, je joue du piano* … (I play the guitar, I play the drums, I play the piano…)

13. Gigi et Georges   page 58
Ask your pupils to draw a storyboard or comic strip of Gigi and Georges.

Can the pupils think of another unlikely pair of animal friends? Ask them to draw a picture, come up with names for their animals and then write a sentence: « *X et Y sont amis* » (X and Y are friends).

14. Chloé et Barnabé   page 62
Take the pupils on a walk in a line around the corridors/classroom/gardens. The teacher gives an instruction «*en marchant* », « *en sautant* », « *en dansant* » and the pupils must continue to follow the teacher using the movement that has been given. Ask a volunteer to be the teacher and call out the instructions.

15. Du lundi au dimanche   page 66
Call out different lines from the song and pupils have to do the action to go with that line; e.g. « *mercredi, je fais du ski* » (skiing). When the pupils get good at it, just say the day of the week in French (i.e. leave out the action) and see if they can remember.

Ask a pupil to volunteer acting out an activity from the song and the rest of the class have to call out which day of the week it represents.

Ask pupils to come up with their own list of activities they would do on each day of the week. This would coincide nicely with a topic on sports and hobbies, or pupils could use dictionaries to look up the vocabulary they need.

16. Papy, raconte-moi une histoire !   page 70
Split the class into small groups. Provide them with simple story books in French and ask them to read a page or so each to the other pupils.

The teacher draws an image on the board and the pupils have to guess which line from the song the teacher has tried to illustrate. After a couple of rounds, put the pupils into pairs and get them to repeat the activity. The person guessing must say the line in French.

17. Une glace à la vanille page 74
Ask the pupils to design and label their own ice cream. Brainstorm the vocabulary for cherries, strawberries, nuts, chocolate chips, raspberry sauce, etc. Ask them to write a paragraph describing their ice creams (including colours and flavours). Teach them the phrase « *C'est délicieux !* » This would make a great wall display.

18. Le rap du hérisson page 78
Split the class into four groups and assign each group a different verse from the rap. Each group must then make up their actions and act out their verse in their own way. For example, they may decide to say one line each and then all join in on the last line, or they may decide to say the whole verse in unison. The class then has a 'rap party', where each group shows the rest of the class how they have arranged their verse. This could even be made into a competition with points awarded for creativity, pronunciation, teamwork etc.

Challenge: can pupils translate the sentences they created in exercise 2 (on page 81) into English?

19. Qu'est-ce que ... ? page 82
Working in pairs or small groups, ask pupils to change the lyrics of the song to describe other activities for today, yesterday and tomorrow. Pupils will be able to use the same tense constructions (*je* + verb conjugated in the present tense, *j'ai* + past participle, *je vais* + infinitive) and simply change the activity, and/or the person they are doing the activity with, e.g: « *je joue au rugby avec mon père* » (I play rugby with my dad). Ideas can be brainstormed on the board before pupils break off into pairs/groups. Ask for volunteers to read out their sentences to the rest of the class.

On the lyric sheet, pupils could draw lines from the pictures to the relevant verses.

20. Trois oiseaux page 86
Use this song as an opportunity to discuss other animals and mini-beasts you might find in the garden. Which animal would the pupils like to be? Pupils could draw and label a picture, then write a sentence using a template: « *Je voudrais être... un escargot/une araignée/un écureuil* », etc.

21. Le petit canard Coin-coin page 90
One pupil is chosen to leave the room. Another student hides a plastic duck. The pupil is called back into the room and tasked with finding the missing duck. The other pupils can help by remaining silent if the pupil is nowhere near the duck, or by saying « *coin-coin* » if they are getting closer. The pupils chanting « *coin-coin* » will get louder the closer the 'finder' gets to discovering the duck!

Translation of assessment phrases on worksheets and Powerpoint

Song no.	Page	French	English
1	12	Bonjour petit lapin brun !	Hello little brown rabbit!
2	16	J'ai un gros cachalot dans mon seau !	I have a big whale in my bucket!
3	20	Mon petit loup joue avec le hibou dans la gadoue.	My little wolf is playing with the owl in the mud.
4	24	Il y a une araignée dans ma baignoire.	There is a spider in my bathtub.
5	28	Lulu la tortue joue au foot sur Neptune.	Lulu the turtle is playing football on Neptune.
6	32	Le cochon mange des bonbons et le lion joue du violon !	The pig is eating sweets and the lion is playing the violin.
7	36	Mon ami Julien aimerait un petit chien.	My friend Julien would like a little dog.
8	40	Le chat en chocolat boit un chocolat chaud !	The chocolate cat is drinking a hot chocolate.
9	44	La petite bête pète sur ma tête !	The little bug is trumping on my head.
10	48	Le petit enfant aime sa maman.	The little child loves her mummy.
11	52	Le caleçon de François le serpent tombe !	The boxer shorts of François the snake are falling down!
12	56	Gaston le gorille porte des godasses dorées pour jouer de la guitare.	Gaston the gorilla wears gold trainers to play the guitar.
	57 (Worksheet B)	Gaston le gorille aime jouer de la guitare.	Gaston the gorilla likes to play the guitar.
13	60	Gigi la girafe et Georges le rouge-gorge sont amis.	Gigi the giraffe and Georges the robin are friends.
14	64	Je voudrais aller à l'école en fusée avec Chloé et Barnabé !	I would like to go to school by rocket with Chloe and Barnaby.
15	68	Youpi ! C'est Samedi ! Je peux rester au lit !	Hooray! It's Saturday! I can stay in bed!
16	72	Le roi mange du poisson froid avec des petits pois !	The king is eating cold fish with peas!
17	76	Toutes les filles dans ma famille mangent des glaces à la vanille !	All the girls in my family eat vanilla ice cream!
18	80	Hervé le hérisson va à l'hôpital en hélicoptère.	Harvey the hedgehog is going to hospital in a helicopter.
	81 (Worksheet B)	Hervé le hérisson a hâte de hiberner cet hiver avec Harry le hamster.	Harvey the hedgehog can't wait to hibernate this winter with Harry the hamster.

Song no.	Page	French	English
19	84	Qu'est-ce que tu fais pour ton anniversaire ? Qui vient à ta fête ?	What are you doing for your birthday? Who is coming to your party?
20	88	Les oiseaux mangent les fraises, les cerises et les raisins dans mon jardin.	The birds eat the strawberries, the cherries and the grapes in my garden.
21	92	En allant trop loin, Coin-coin s'est perdu dans le foin !	By venturing too far, Quack-quack got lost in the hay!

Translation of word lists on Powerpoint

Song no.	Grapheme	Words in the song		Other words	
		French	English	French	English
1	un	un brun quelqu'un	one brown anybody	lundi jungle	Monday jungle
2	o/eau	cachalot gros eau beau seau	whale fat/big water handsome bucket	robot stylo bateau cadeau chapeau	robot pen boat gift hat
3	ou	loup où doux joue nous tout hibou gadoue chouette toujours	wolf where soft play we all owl mud great always	douche poule bijou genou souris	shower chicken jewel knee mouse
4	gn	araignée mignon baignoire	spider cute bathtub	cygne campagne lasagnes montagne champignon	swan countryside lasagna mountain mushroom
5	u	Lulu tortue lune sur fusée Neptune revenue univers	Lulu turtle moon on rocket Neptune came back universe	bus jupe pull lunettes nuage peluche	bus skirt jumper glasses cloud cuddly toy

Song no.	Grapheme	Words in the song		Other words	
		French	English	French	English
6	on	cochon mouton lion poisson hérisson mignon bonbons gazon violon pantalon avion	pig sheep lion fish hedgehog cute sweets grass violin trousers plane	ballon maison savon camion papillon confiture	ball house soap truck butterfly jam
7	ien	chien bien rien Julien	dog good nothing Julien	ancien combien gardien italien magicien	ancient how much guardian Italian magician
8	ch	chat chaud chasser chocolat	cat hot to chase chocolate	chambre château chameau cochon pêche	bedroom castle camel pig fishing
9	ê/è	bête fête tête pète	bug party head trump	crêpe rêve forêt frère mère très	pancake/crêpe dream forest brother mother very
10	en/an	enfant grand maman demande	child big mummy ask	en dent menthe tente vendredi chanter manger janvier orange pantalon	in tooth mint tent Friday to sing to eat January orange trousers
11	ç/s/ss	caleçon François garçons serpent essaye	boxer shorts François boys snake try	français leçon balançoire souris sucre dessin poussin	French lesson swing mouse sugar drawing chick

Song no.	Grapheme	Words in the song		Other words	
		French	English	French	English
12	go/ga/gu	gorille godasses Gaston guitare fatigué	gorilla shoes Gaston guitar tired	gare galette gâteau gomme rigolo guichet guirlande	station galette cake rubber funny ticket office garland
13	gi/ge/gé	girafe Gigi Georges rouge-gorge géante	giraffe Gigi George robin giant (f)	bougie magie gilet genou génial	candle magic vest knee awesome
14	é/er	fée Chloé Barnabé fusée éléphant école vélo aller	fairy Chloe Barnaby rocket elephant school bike to go	bébé étoile musée araignée jouer manger regarder écouter	baby star museum spider to play to eat to look to listen
15	i	lundi mardi mercredi jeudi vendredi samedi dimanche lit riz ski fruits merci amis différent	Monday Tuesday Wednesday Thursday Friday Saturday Sunday bed rice skiing fruit thank you friends different	brioche fille kiwi lion Paris petit	brioche girl kiwi lion Paris little
16	oi	histoire moi toi loi bois rois quoi froid noir couloir étoile	story me you law forest kings what cold black hallway star	poisson croissant voici oiseau baignoire	fish croissant here bird bathtub

Song no.	Grapheme	Words in the song		Other words	
		French	English	French	English
17	ille	**brille** **filles** **famille** **vanille**	shine girls family vanilla	**bille** **gorille** **chenille**	marble gorilla caterpillar
18	silent h	**hélicoptère** **hamster** **hippo** **hérisson** **histoire** **hamburger** **hôpital** **Hervé** **Hector** **Harry**	helicopter hamster hippo hedgehog story hamburger hospital Harvey Hector Harry	**huit** **herbe** **hibou** **hiver** **heureux** **haricot**	eight herb owl winter happy bean
19	qu	**qu'est-ce que** **qui** **quel** **quand** **pourquoi**	what who which when why	**quinze** **question** **quitter** **requin** **mostique**	fifteen question to leave shark mosquito
20	s sounds like z	**oiseaux** **fraises** **raisins** **cerises** **bise** **troisième** **trois oiseaux** **vous êtes** **vos ailes**	birds strawberries grapes cherries kiss third three birds you are your wings	**maison** **framboise** **nous avons** **vous avez**	house raspberry we have you (pl) have
21	oin	**Coin-coin** **foin** **loin** **besoin**	Quack-quack hay far need	**moins** **point** **soin** **témoin**	less point care witness

Answers

1. Il y a quelqu'un ?   page 13

Ex2. <u>jun</u>gle = jungle
<u>lun</u>di = Monday
br<u>un</u> = brown
chac<u>un</u> = each
<u>un</u> = one/a/an

Ex3. Illustrations of: a little purple rabbit; a little green horse; a little blue bird

Ex4. <u>u</u>n   s<u>i</u>x
d<u>eu</u>x   s<u>e</u>pt
tr<u>oi</u>s   h<u>ui</u>t
quatr<u>e</u>   n<u>eu</u>f
c<u>i</u>nq   d<u>i</u>x

2. Mon cachalot   page 17

Ex2. **gros** (fat), **stylo** (pen), **dos** (back), **mot** (word)

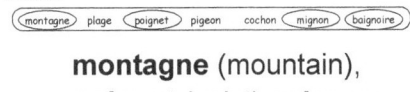

Ex3. **couteau** (knife), **bateau** (boat), **beau** (beautiful), **chapeau** (hat)

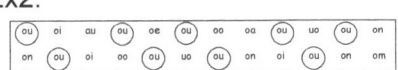

Ex4. **cachalot** (sperm whale)

3. Mon petit loup   page 21
Ex2.

| ou | oi | au | ou | oe | ou | oo | oa | ou | uo | ou | on |
| on | ou | oi | oo | ou | uo | ou | on | oi | ou | on | om |

9

Ex3. l<u>ou</u>p = wolf
hib<u>ou</u> = owl
b<u>ou</u>les = boules
gad<u>ou</u>e = mud

Ex4.

fourmi	souris	journal	tortue
poule	bateau	douche	boîte
amour	bonbon	soupe	route

fourmi (ant), **souris** (mouse), **journal** (newspaper), **poule** (hen), **douche** (shower), **amour** (love), **soupe** (soup), **route** (road)

8

4. Une araignée dans ma baignoire   page 25

Ex2.

montagne plage poignet pigeon cochon mignon baignoire
(circled: montagne, poignet, mignon, baignoire)

montagne (mountain), **poignet** (wrist), **mignon** (cute), **baignoire** (bathtub)

5. Lulu la tortue   page 29

None.

6. Le rock 'n' rock du cochon   page 33

Ex2. **cochon** (pig), **mouton** (sheep), **lion** (lion), **poisson** (fish), **hérisson** (hedgehog)

Ex3. **bonbon** = sweet
gazon = grass lawn
violon = violin
pantalon = trousers
avion = aeroplane

Ex3. Illustrations of: a pig eating sweets; a fish wearing a pair of trousers; a hedgehog piloting an aeroplane.

7. Mon ami Julien   page 37

Ex2.

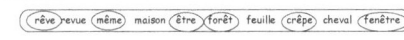

chien (dog), **rien** (nothing), **bien** (good), **magicien** (magician)

Ex3. Illustrations of: penguin; baboon; shark

8. Le chat en chocolat page 41

Ex2. **pas** (not), **rat** (rat), **chocolat** (chocolate)

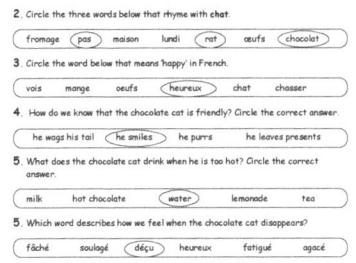

Ex3. **heureux**
Ex4. he smiles
Ex5. water
Ex6. **déçu** (disappointed)
Ex7. Illustrations of: he eats eggs; he is smiling at me; he is too hot.

9. Il y a une petite bête   page 45

Ex2.

rêve (dream), **même** (same), **être** (to be), **forêt** (forest), **crêpe** (crepe), **fenêtre** (window)

Ex3.

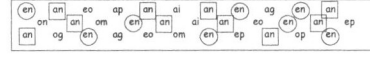

Ex4. Illustrations of bug on the head: singing; jumping; trumping.

10. Petit enfant   page 49

Ex2.

en	an	eo	ap	an	ai	an	en	ag	en	ap
on	an	om	en	an	ai	an	eo	en	ep
an	og	en	ag	eo	om	en	ep	an	ap	en

circles = 8
squares = 10

11. François le serpent page 53
Ex2.

Ex3. **serpent** (snake), **garçon** (boy), **caleçon** (boxer shorts)

12. Gaston le gorille page 57
Ex2.

garçon (boy), **guerre** (war), **gomme** (rubber), **goûter** (snack), **gagner** (to win)

Ex3. **goûter** = snack
guitare = guitar
gorille = gorilla
godasse = shoe

13. Gigi et Georges page 61
Ex2.

grand (big) **petit** (small)
froid (cold) **chaud** (hot)
rapide (fast) **lent** (slow)
jeune (young) **vieux** (old)
plein (full) **vide** (empty)

14. Chloé et Barnabé page 65
Ex2.

éléphant (elephant), **école** (school), **fée** (fairy), **fusée** (rocket), **vélo** (bike)
5

15. Du lundi au dimanche page 69
Ex2. lun**di**
mar**di**
mercre**di**
jeu**di**
vendre**di**
same**di**
dimanche

Ex3. a) **lit** (bed), b) **mange** (eat), c) **ski** (skiing), d) **fruits** (fruit), e) **merci** (thank you), f) **vois** (see)

16. Papy, raconte-moi une histoire ! page 73
Ex2.

histoire (story), **froid** (cold), **noir** (black), **moi** (me)

Ex3. Illustrations of stories about: dragons and kings; a big wolf in the woods; a grandpa telling a story.

Ex4.
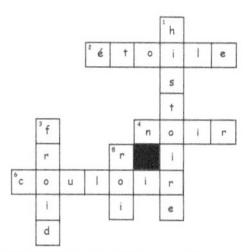

17. Une glace à la vanille page 77
Ex2.

fille (girl), **bille** (marble), **gorille** (gorilla), **cheville** (ankle)

Ex3. **chenille** (caterpillar), **jonquille** (daffodil), **gorille** (gorilla), **famille** (family)

Ex4. **menthe** (mint) = green
citron (lemon) = yellow
fraise (strawberry) = red
chocolat (chocolate) = brown

18. Le rap du hérisson page 81
None.

19. Qu'est-ce que ... ? page 85
Ex2. Qui = Who
Quand = When
Quel = Which
Où = Where
Comment = How
Est-ce que = Is it that (do you)
Combien = How many
Pourquoi = Why
Qu'est-ce que = What is it that (what do you)

Ex3. Illustrations of: I'm playing football with my friends; I went skateboarding with my brother; I am going to walk my dog

20. Trois oiseaux page 89
Ex2. **trois araignées** = 3 spiders
trois éléphants = 3 elephants
trois hirondelles = 3 swallows

Ex3. In my garden, there are three trees and lots of flowers. There is a snail, two spiders and three birds. There are also four strawberries, five grapes and six cherries.

21. Le petit canard Coin-coin page 93
Ex2.

loin (far), **coin** (corner), **besoin** (need), **témoin** (witness)

Ex3.
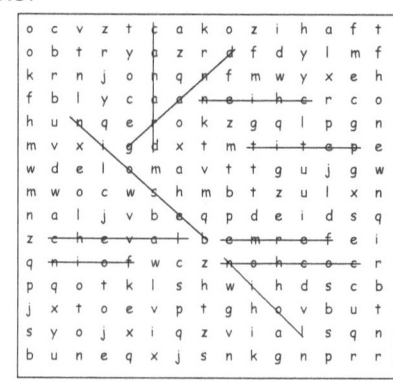

canard (duck), **cheval** (horse), **chien** (dog), **foin** (hay), **loin** (far), **besoin** (need), **cochon** (pig); **petit** (little), **grand** (big), **ferme** (farm)

Ex4. Colour code for illustration:
Coin-coin (duck) = yellow
foin (hay) = brown
cochon (pig) = pink
chien (dog) = black
cheval (horse) = grey

Download instructions

To download your free resources for **21 Fun Songs to Teach French Phonics**:

Go to: https://www.brilliantpublications.education

You will need to set up a log in with an email address and password if you do not already have one for the https://www.brilliantpublications.education website. (Please note: you will need to set up a new account on this website to download your files, even if you already have an account on our main website.)

Your username may contain: **letters**, **numbers** and the special characters * - _ . @

You will be asked to confirm your email address by clicking the validation link emailed to you when you register.

Don't forget to check in spam/junk if you do not see an email from us.

We have introduced 2-factor authorisation on this website to make it more secure. This means that whenever you log in, you will be sent a numerical authorisation code by email which you must copy and paste into the welcome page on the website. The authentication code only lasts 1 hour.

Once logged on, choose the *French* category and click on the cover for *21 Fun Songs to Teach French Phonics*.

Your unique password for the downloads is **AgqLeD9t**.

The downloaded filename will be **21-French-Phonic-Songs.zip**.

Please note, the password will be changed at regular intervals so make sure you save a copy of the files once you have downloaded them.

If you experience any difficulties with downloading your files, please email info@brilliantpublications.co.uk and we will get back to you as soon as possible.

Depending on the speed of your internet and the size of the download, it may take some time for the download to complete. To avoid problems, please make sure that your computer does not go to sleep during the download.

Note: We test the software on PCs and Apple Macs, but there are too many different types of hardware in schools for us to be able to test it on every device owned by schools.

www.ingramcontent.com/pod-product-compliance
Lightning Source LLC
Chambersburg PA
CBHW080902230426
43663CB00013B/2604